LIVE YOUR BEST LIFE

Answer the Call

Dear Sis Bonnie,

Continue to Live Your Best Life. Thank you for Answering the Call and living your life on "Purpose." I thank God for our connection. Truly the I know the Best is Yet to Come!

Love you to Life

[signature]
#blessedgirl

Presented by Ruben West

Copyright © 2017 R. West Enterprises, LLC. All rights reserved.

No part of this publication may be excerpted, reproduced, or transmitted in any form or by means electronic or mechanical, photocopied, or scanned, except as permitted under 107 or 108 of the 1976 United States Copyright Act, or printed for distribution or resale without express written permission from the author.

Published by R. West Enterprises, LLC.

Edited by Alexa Elliott

Printed in the United States of America

Dedication

This book is dedicated to my children, Monica, Spencer, and Robinson; my wife, Robin; my parents, Robert and Rosetta, as well as the rest of my family and friends that continue to encourage me. Thank you for your love and support. Never stop pursuing your dreams.

To Edwina Blackman, RN — although we work together in the surgery department focusing our attention on other people, the biggest operation took place on me. I've heard it said that the hardest thing to open is a closed mind. If that's the case, you are a master surgeon because you helped me to see things in myself that I could not see. I am forever grateful and appreciative for your contribution to my life. The work continues.

To my "Live Your BEST Life" board members and everyone else who believed and continues to believe that together we can make a difference even one life at a time; this book is for you.

— Ruben West

Foreword

When we hear the phrase "answer the call," it's easy to think of a team of firemen hearing the alarm and springing into action, knowing that someone's home, property, and maybe even their very life is at stake.

But think for a minute — what if there were no firemen? What if you were in need of help and there was no one assigned to help you? Can you imagine how devastating that would feel? Unfortunately, there are people that feel that very way and the question is, who is supposed to help them?

These authors discovered that our life assignment, or calling if you will, is much like an assignment in school. The assignment is there to grow you, test your knowledge, and develop you into a better person. Your life assignment may not be easy to carry out or even easy to discover. Fortunately, this team of co-authors came together to give you some strategies that will not only help you figure out your calling, but answer it as well.

Is it easy to walk in your purpose? Not according to the contributors of this manuscript. They masterfully outline how life will shock you, rock you, and even hit you on the blind side. You may even face days where you question if it's even worth it to try and live out your life's mission. In those hard times and on those difficult days, you are being transformed from the coal to the diamond, from the caterpillar to the butterfly, from the everyday citizen to the firemen committed to risking it all to help someone else.

If you know someone who is looking for steps to get their life back on track, those steps are in this book. If you're looking for strategies to overcome personal setbacks, they are in this book. If you or someone you know would like to turn up the heat and live life on purpose and on fire while carrying out your life's mission, continue reading this book.

When it comes down to it, I think we all have a calling on our lives. At some point, we all hear the proverbial "ringing of the phone." You can hear it and choose to not answer, but just remember, life wasn't calling for your benefit. Life calls out to you just like the alarm calls out to the firemen at the station. Someone is in need! Someone needs your skills, gifts, talents, abilities, and more. Join me on this journey to personal accountability as these transparent, authentic, and brave individuals share their stories and give concrete steps on how you too can Answer the Call.

— **Ruben West**

TABLE OF CONTENTS

Chapter 1
Trust the Dream Giver   9
By Susan Gibson

Chapter 2
Believe in the Dream   14
By Susan Gibson
Biography — Susan Gibson   19

Chapter 3
A Two-and-a-Half Month Second   22
By Jeff Marconette

Chapter 4
Make It Count   31
By Jeff Marconette
Biography — Jeff Marconette   37

Chapter 5
There's Always Tomorrow   39
By Dr. Adria E. Luster

Chapter 6
Live for Today!   60
By Dr. Adria E. Luster
Biography — Dr. Adria E. Luster   81

Chapter 7
Walking Through the Darkness   82
By Rhonda Kohler

Chapter 8
Redeeming Grace   88
By Rhonda Kohler
Biography — Rhonda Kohler   99

Chapter 9
Created on Purpose for a Purpose **100**
By Rosha Chandler

Chapter 10
Closing the Gap **109**
By Rosha Chandler
Biography — Rosha Chandler **115**

Chapter 11
Move Forward... And Don't Look Back **116**
By Angie Hodges

Chapter 12
Shine Bright **126**
By Angie Hodges
Biography — Angie Hodges **137**

Chapter 13
We Are Inadequate... Aren't We? **139**
By Cori Briggs

Chapter 14
We Are Powerful Beyond Measure **152**
By Cori Briggs
Biography — Cori Briggs **165**

Chapter 15
Roller Coaster of Pain **166**
By Rosetta West

Chapter 16
Never Let Go of Hope **182**
By Rosetta West
Biography — Rosetta West **189**

Chapter 17
Faith Over Fear **191**

By Anana Phifer-Derilhomme

Chapter 18
You are an Overcomer **201**
By Anana Phifer-Derilhomme
Biography — Anana Phifer-Derilhomme **212**

Chapter 19
Midnight **214**
By Robin Cody Smith

Chapter 20
How to Overcome an Unexpected Loss **223**
By Robin Cody Smith
Biography — Robin Cody Smith **231**

Trust the Dream Giver
Susan Gibson

"We know He causes all things to work together for our good for those who love Him and are called according to His purpose." — Romans 8:28

For the past few years, I have been hit with serious and unique health issues that have almost kept me from my calling. Approximately three years ago, I developed a severe case of psoriasis on both my hands and feet, which made it difficult to walk and be around people. The skin on both my hands and feet literally was peeling off. Each time I walked, the pressure of my body caused the skin on my feet to crack, leaving me with deep crevices on both my extremities. It looked like modern day leprosy.

The following summer, while in the emergency room dealing with an unrelated issue, I developed a severe case of what was diagnosed as Bell's palsy. The left side of my face became paralyzed, affecting my vision and my speech. At the time, I was working as a professor in communications at a local university. Facing this medical challenge as a speech professor one week before the start of the semester was more than a major nuisance. Additionally, I had recently joined the "Black Belt" Speakers group. I found the entire situation ironic.

Functioning in my expected rolls became extremely difficult, and I was encouraged to take a medical leave. However, I decided not to choose a permanent solution to a temporary situation. I struggled, but I made it through the school year.

Finally, the school year had come to an end. Thank God. I was exhausted, but I made it. I had pushed myself all year. I was determined to rest that summer and possibly do some writing after an inspiring and motivating Black Belt Conference where God reinforced the call He has on my life. I was determined more than ever to get my health back on track, write, and develop my message. This was April. By May, I had been diagnosed with pancreatic cancer — my life was about to change in ways I had never imagined.

The cancer diagnosis turned my entire world upside down. Everything prior to that announcement ceased to be important. All plans to move forward went into a holding pattern. It was as though someone cancelled summer. Cancer was the new center of our lives.

I had just accepted a radio interview on my upcoming book, entitled *Are You Getting Your Rest? Release Your Expectations, Surrender, and Trust God.* To my disappointment, the radio interview had to be put on hold. But I was about to about to take my own advice. I could only rest, release my expectations, surrender, and trust my God.

My daughter was to be an incoming freshman, and we made plans to shop for her new dorm room and do all the things parents do for a first-time college student. I was unable to do any of those things; I had to rely on family friends to help. My son had just finished his associate's degree and was transferring to a four-year university. I wanted to take a tour, which was cancelled. My husband was finally settling into his new job and we put our house on the market. All plans to move forward with this new stage of life were put on hold. We had to take our house off the market because I needed somewhere to stay while embarking on the healing process.

This challenge, or as some may say obstacle, affected me in many ways. I must start by saying, "I love what I do." Teaching is very fulfilling, not only emotionally, but also personally. Especially given the subject matter — speech. Many times, when I would tell people what I did for a living, they would say, "I hated speech." My standard response was, "That is because you did not have me as an instructor." Making a difference in the lives of young people is key to who I am, and now that seemed to be in jeopardy. The barrage of difficulties even called my sense of identity into question. On top of all this, there were the physical effects of cancer. There was a cancerous tumor on my pancreas. I would have to prepare for chemotherapy, radiation, and ultimately, I would need surgery to remove the head of my pancreas, gallbladder, and a section of my small intestine. Apparently, as far as cancer goes, pancreatic cancer is a tough one to beat.

One of the hardest things to deal with was an overwhelming feeling of helplessness. I am someone who plans for the future, and it seemed like it was no longer an option. Worst yet, there was nothing I could do about it. There were people depending on me. I needed to be strong. Terms like chemotherapy, radiation, and surgery dominated our conversation. My own death was a real possibility.

Right now, you may say, "I'm not dealing with a health diagnosis." However, you may be going through something that possesses a similar set of challenges. For example, the death of a loved one. I have met many people who have experienced this and have been unable to move forward. Even when they relay the story, it sounds as though it was yesterday, and they are stuck feeling overwhelmed and helpless. They've become hostage to grief, frustrated because it seems there isn't anything they can do to bring them back. Unfortunately, they remain unable to move forward.

During my crisis, I had to stop focusing on other's interpretation of my "reality." I needed to know what the purpose of this trial was, or should I say opportunity? I was convinced I was entering a new and exciting season of my life. I saw a lot of the Promises of God coming together. New opportunities, new doors, and new levels of maturity surrounded me. Everyone wants the testimony, but no one wants the test. Like it or not, the test was here. I was intentional when I communicated the situation. I presented it as an opportunity for God to show up. My husband, children, family, and friends were on the same page regarding the outcome. I didn't allow anyone who doubted God to come into my personal circle. I hand-picked those who came to visit, and I texted reports of the victories along the way.

Probably one of the hardest things was to allow those who loved and cared about me to help. I'm so used to doing it myself.

Believe in the Dream
Susan Gibson

"But what does it say? 'The word is near you; it is in your mouth and in your heart,' that is, the message concerning the faith that we proclaim." — Romans 10:8 NIV

When facing various trials of life, we often feel that our solutions are so far out of reach. We go to great lengths looking to experts, seeking the opinions of others, and browsing through every possible online source in search of answers. While all of that has its proper place, I found that simply believing in the dream that God had placed inside of me yielded the most powerful results. I learned a truth that I share now. What you think you are missing, you already have inside of you.

I had known from my childhood that I possessed a unique ability to use my voice to encourage and inspire others. I had been internally equipped with a type of boldness and have always valued truth over a lie, regardless of the cost of speaking it. Even as a little girl, I would envision myself speaking to large audiences in a way that greatly impacted them for good.

When I found myself facing cancer, it was believing in that childhood, God-given dream that began to change things. Don't get me wrong. My experience, diagnosis, pain, and challenges didn't disappear. The change was in the way that I was able to deal with it all. I had to have a different point of focus. I chose the promise, the dream that God had given me. I believe with every fiber that it is yet to be fulfilled and that I will live to see it fully manifested!

Perhaps the answer on the inside of you is different from mine. Maybe you have been gifted with an amazing ability to sing, or you have a creative knack for building things. Whatever the case may be, the answer to some of your most pressing challenges is already on the inside of you. Unpacking that gift and using it to overcome the obstacles you face is as simple as **speaking** it. Let me explain.

Simply Believe:
Believe that you are created for greatness. Speaking that truth out loud is key. Say to yourself, "I know there is great treasure on the inside of me." "I believe I was created with tremendous purpose and potential." The Bible tells us that we are who we think we are in our heart. Speaking the truth out loud can help you eventually believe it in your heart.

Present Your Proof:
Provide proof you were created with seeds of greatness. For this type of proof, you must turn to the one who knows you best; God the Creator. His word is filled with proof of who you are and what He put in you. Here are a couple examples that I found and used.

"Before I formed you in the womb I knew you, before you were born I set you apart, I appointed you a prophet to the nations." — Jeremiah 1:5 (NIV)

"You saw me before I was born. Every day of my life was recorded in your book. Every moment was laid out before a single day had passed." — Psalms 139:16 (NLT)

Expect Opportunities to Manifest Greatness:
Reframe the way you see things. As long as I believed my diagnosis to be a death sentence, I could feel myself becoming more and more anxious and discouraged. After seeking God regarding the purpose for this unexpected season, I realized that He was simply setting the stage, creating a platform, and providing opportunities for my gift to be use in ways I had never imagined. With this mindset, I began looking more at the special opportunities in my circumstances.

One day in particular, on one of my many trips to the medical center in Chicago, I realized that I would was very near to a church of some pastor friends. I stopped in and God allowed me to speak a much-needed word of encouragement to them. Looking back, I realize that I never would have even encountered them if I had not been coming there to deal with my own sickness.

Accept the Challenge:
In other words, "just do it." Start exercising your gift or talent. I remember a day when about 40 of my closest friends had all gathered at my home to offer encouragement and support. By the strength of God, I too found courage and strength to speak life and encouragement to each one of them. I knew there was something on the inside of me that would send a spark of life to something inside of them.

If your gift is poetry, write an encouragement card to someone. If God has gifted you with a special skill for cooking, make a pot of chicken noodle soup for someone else in need. Just doing the thing that you are good at and passionate about will change things for you and others.

Keep a Record of Your Victories:

Let your victories establish a foundation to build upon. When David, the shepherd boy who eventually became King of Israel, was faced with the giant Goliath, he found strength in reflecting back on former victories. "Your servant has killed both the lion and the bear," David reported to King Saul. Then David confidently declared that Goliath would suffer the same fate.

We too can benefit from keeping a record of past victories when facing our current challenges. I found that journaling is a practical and helpful way to accomplish this. When we keep a record of our victories as well as our challenges, we can actually see the changes and note the processes that brought them about. Our victory record not only becomes strength and hope for us in a future challenge, but as I hope is true with this book, our victories can help someone else find hope and encouragement.

I hope by now that you are convinced that every single human being was created with seeds of greatness inside. This greatness doesn't just accidently leak out. You must actively unlock it and the words of your mouth are the key.

That one word, "SPEAK," has become the message of my life. I've learned that when I am silent, my greatness fails to be manifested. I focus on my fears, inabilities, and insecurities. But when I speak, especially speaking the Word of God, speaking positive truths that I see in others, or even speaking hope for a dismal-looking situation of my own, things change and they change for the better.

Susan M. Gibson

Susan Maxine Gibson is a graduate of State University of New York at Buffalo with a Masters of Arts degree in Organizational Training and Development, Bachelors of Art degree in Interpersonal/Intercultural Communications, and Certification in Public Relations/Advertising. In 1998, Mrs. Gibson was hired as an Instructional Assistant Professor in the School of Communication at Illinois State University. Susan has received numerous awards, including the Outstanding Faculty Award from the Office of Intercultural Programs and Services and Certificates of Appreciation from the Office of Residential Life at Illinois State University, where she is a Faculty Mentor. Prior to this position, she was an Academic Counselor for special programs designed to help first generation students complete a four-year degree.

She has presented in statewide conferences and workshops on a variety of communication issues, such as effective customer service enhancement, communicating across barriers, and getting your point across for University of Illinois in Springfield. She has contracted with Illinois Wesleyan University for an annual day-long communication workshop for minority honor students. During this workshop, she addresses issues such as professional imagining, intercultural communication, conflict resolution, and public speaking. A major part of the services includes a personalized curriculum development, group facilitation, and an individualized critique of workshop participants.

In addition to developing students, Mrs. Gibson has strong community ties. Susan has partnered with various groups such as the Jack and Jill organization in Normal, IL to provide speaking opportunities for our youth. In their annual Speak-Up for Success, students ranging from 1st to 12th grade are introduced to the speaking arena, including research, technology implementation, and formal presentation. She has been a guest presenter at Heartland Community College's Business Essentials; a program geared towards training nontraditional students preparing to reenter the workforce regarding the necessary skills for successful reentry.

Susan has received invitations from area companies desiring to improve communication effectiveness. Most recently, she was contacted by Definitive Neuro-Diagnostics offices, of Normal, IL, a surgical monitoring company. While a small company, it offers a variety of positions ranging from technical support, customer service, sales, education and development, and a unique multicultural/international mix, which posed a variety of communication challenges. After evaluating the needs of the company, she was able to design a workshop to identify the communication styles of key department heads, illustrated how they interacted within the company, and developed strategies for enhancement.

Currently, as a board member of the Habitat for Humanity,

McLean County division, Susan has had the opportunity to conduct training on teambuilding, effective communication, and problem-solving.

Susan is a devout Christian and believes we were all created with purpose.

Susan, her children, and her husband reside in Normal, IL.

A Two-and-a-Half Month Second
Jeff Marconette

"Impossible is nothing." — Muhammad Ali

The Moment in Time That Changed My Life

Have you ever had someone tell you that you can't do something? Well, how about being 17-years-old and having people tell you that you'd never walk again? How would you take that news? Would you sit there and take it, or would you stand up and prove them wrong?

The moment in time that changed my life forever happened on January 7, 2002. I was 17 years old, a junior in high school, and I was on my way to get some lunch. This was a lunch I'd never get to, because my life was about to change in an instant. I don't even remember anything that happened past that morning, so everything I know about this incident was told to me after the fact.

I was stopped at the red light, waiting for it to turn green. I'm told that the car behind me honked, so I pulled out into the intersection. At that exact moment, a semi-truck coming from the other direction ran the red light, t-boning my car in the middle of the intersection. I was immediately knocked unconscious by the impact of it slamming into the driver's side of my car. The police were unable to even tell how fast the semi-truck driver was going. They explained that the driver never hit his brakes, so there were no skid marks to measure to determine the speed at the time the truck hit my car.

I have no memory of any of this! The next thing I knew, I woke up in the hospital. What felt like a second in time to me was actually 2 ½ months later! I'd been in a coma, and I remember nothing from the morning of the accident to waking up at Miami Valley Hospital.

Because I'd been T-boned by a semi-truck, things weren't looking good for me. The first thing the doctors and nurses had to do was stabilize me from life-threatening injuries, so I was in the trauma ward for eleven days. I had a broken jaw, two fractured ribs, a punctured lung, and a ruptured spleen. They performed a tracheotomy and put a tube through my neck to help me breathe. I'd been on a ventilator for a few days, and the doctors also put a tube through the side of my chest to re-inflate my lung and a g-tube (feeding tube) in my stomach. The most significant result of my accident was that it left me with a traumatic brain injury, which would change my life forever.

My occipital condyles — the two rounded knobs that form the joint with my first cervical vertebra — were broken, and doctors put me in a halo for three months. A halo is a way to keep your head and neck still while you get better after an accident. The doctors drilled four screws into my skull, and there were four posts going up, and a halo around my head — like an angel. One time, one of the screws on the halo came loose, so they had to use a special wrench to tighten it back down to my skull. It was the worst pressure I've ever felt! I was a tough kid, but having them tighten it down to my skull made me cry, especially because they couldn't give me pain medication until *after* the halo was tightened. The halo also weighed 20 pounds, which meant that while I was relearning how to walk, I was doing it while carrying a 20-pound weight that was screwed into my head!

Starting Over Again

Before my accident, I was your average 17-year-old kid. I went to school, spent time with my friends, and I was an avid BMX bike rider. I rode whenever I possibly could — 24/7, 365 days a year. I loved being out on my bike. I'd started out racing bikes, and eventually moved onto riding on the streets. After that, I started riding park and street park, which involves a lot of grinding, technical tricks, aerial tricks, wall rides, and more. We used to go all over my home state of Ohio, always finding new places to ride.

No matter where we went, I found time and ways to ride, including a time when a friend and I brought our bikes on vacation with my family to Clearwater Beach, Florida. No matter the location or season, I was out on my bike. In the summer, we rode 18-20 miles a day on country roads and going for distance. Once, after an ice storm, my friends and I found a way to make snow tires for our BMX bikes. We did this by taking old bike tires and hammering nails out of them so the nails were facing outward, creating traction on the ice. There was a good three inches of ice on the road, and we rode with our hand-made snow tires. In hindsight, it might not have been the safest choice, but we did it and we had fun.

Your whole life has to start over after experiencing a traumatic or dramatic event. When I came out of the coma and woke up in the hospital, I had to relearn how to walk, how to talk, how to eat, and how to drink. Even though I'd turned 17 just a few months before the accident on October 12, I had to start over as if I were born again. All the stuff you and I learned as a baby, I had to relearn. I had to start over from scratch, and it wasn't easy. Once I was able to leave the ICU, I was moved to a step-down unit, and after that, a rehab ward at the hospital. While in the hospital, I received extensive therapies, including speech, physical, occupational, and recreational.

At first, I thought my dreams were dead as a result of my accident. I had aspirations to be a professional BMX rider, to go into the military and serve my country, and to become a mechanical engineer. After that fateful day on January 7, none of those dreams worked for me anymore. I soon realized that just as I was starting over and growing in a different direction, my dreams had to grow and change, too. My dreams weren't dead — they were changing right along with me.

Some people told me recovery would be impossible. I had people telling me that I'd never walk again. Rather than give into the cycle of negative thinking, I laughed and said, "Watch me!" During the time where I was relearning how to walk, talk, eat, and drink, I leaned on my parents and the amazing hospital staff. My parents have helped me immensely through all of this, and they were my biggest source of strength to lean on. In fact, my mom and dad were so incredible that they *never* left me alone at the hospital — not even once.

Fortunately, my dad is a realtor, so he was able to define his working hours. After my accident, he simply informed his office that he wasn't coming in, and he and my mom stayed by my side. My dad was there on the weekdays — day and night. My mom would come down in the evenings, after work, and spent the nights on the weekends. Her boss had generously given her the first month off after my accident, but after that, she had to go back to work. My mom's job was very important, because it was what provided our health insurance — the insurance that kept me in the hospital for a record amount of time. That's what was needed to save my life and get me on the path to recovery. I'd been in that hospital for longer than anyone else before me. Throughout my long stay at the hospital, my parents were always there for me.

The hospital staff were also supportive during my time recovering and relearning how to do basic things that the accident took from me. One of my doctors once told my parents, "We have good nurses in this hospital. We have good doctors and good patient care technicians, and your son will be well taken care of. So you can go on home, but if it was my son, I wouldn't leave, either." Having doctors, nurses, and other hospital staff who look at you as a person, and not just a patient, makes a huge difference when you're in the recovery process. In fact, I had a physical therapist who fully believed in me, to the point that he gave me an extra hour of physical therapy every day, free of charge. He saw that I was just as committed to my recovery as he was, so he saw me twice a day when he only saw other people once a day, and made no extra money as a result. I wanted to get back to normal, and he wanted to help me get there. I'm so grateful for each and every person I encountered at that hospital.

Discovering My New Normal

After my accident and waking up at the hospital, my main goal was just to get back to normal as quickly as I could. I wanted to feel like I was normal again. I've always been a persistent, driven, and determined person, like my momma, and that was my driving force through this whole process. I was going to beat this, and no one was going to stand in my way.

That's not to say that I didn't still experience periods of anger or sadness, especially in the beginning. Like I said, I was an avid BMX rider, which I could no longer do, and that was a big shock to me. I lost some friends along the way as well. Some people just went by the wayside after my accident. Not everyone can adjust with you as you create your new normal, and there were a few friends who disappeared. Some friends, however, remained there for me. I have a really good friend who owns a bike shop in my town, and he's really handy with metal. He made heavy-duty training wheels for me, and I was actually the first person to ride their bike inside Miami Valley Hospital!

Before I could ride a bike, however, I first had to re-learn how to walk, among other things. From January 7th onward, I missed the rest of my junior year of high school. Determined to not be left behind, I made up the rest of my junior year over the summer, which meant I got to start my senior year on time with the rest of my class. I had to go through part of my senior year of high school in a wheel chair. After that, I was able to walk with a walker or cane, and eventually, with nothing at all. In fact, the most significant moment when I walked with nothing was at graduation. Yes, not only did I graduate high school on time, I walked across the stage, with a friend's help, to a standing ovation from the crowd — teachers, parents, classmates, friends, and more.

I will say this: I am definitely a success story, and not everyone has been as fortunate as I was. I know that there are people who have experienced trauma and never come out from it. While my life took a different course than the one I expected, and I had to relearn many basic things, I have my life. My parents told me that while I was in the hospital, there was another patient there near my age who wasn't so fortunate. He was also in high school at the time… the hospital staff called his friends in, and they lined the hospital hallway to say goodbye before he was pulled off life support.

Life doesn't slow down for those of us who are left living it, and it makes things very difficult when you're recovering from a traumatic event. If you're being held back, you're being held back, but life still goes on. That's why I've adopted an attitude of "join me or get out of my way and watch me, because *nothing* will stop me!"

I'll admit that it's taken me a long time to be this positive. I've always had a decent attitude, even happy-go-lucky, but there were times where it was a struggle to stay positive in the face of so many drastic obstacles. There was a period in my life where I dealt with my problems by drinking them away. I was drunk every night of the week, Monday through Sunday. But, like I said, I realized that my dreams weren't dead — they just had to change and grow with me. I changed my attitude back to my positive, happy-go-lucky self by listening to motivational people such as Eric Thomas and Les Brown. Remember, no matter what you do or how hard you try to avoid it, there will always be bad things in life. But it's not the bad things that happen that matter — it's *how you react* to them that makes your life turn out a certain way.

I had a friend tell me once that 14 ½ years ago, he never would have expected to have me sitting at the dinner table with him. He never expected that I'd be where I am today, and I find that very thought provoking. Yes, I was in a terrible accident that left me with broken bones, damaged organs, and a traumatic brain injury, but that wasn't the end of my story! Even after I was discharged from the hospital, I've been back numerous times. I went to outpatient rehab at Miami Valley Hospital's Comprehensive Outpatient Rehabilitation Program, or CORP for short. I was there five days a week, doing physical, occupational, and speech therapy. Today, I receive neurological development therapy from a physical therapist who's certified in working with people with brain injuries, and she helps me out a lot.

Writing is one of the hardest things for me to do. I was originally right-handed, but ever since I was in the accident, my right hand gets really bad tremors. Because of that, whenever I try to do anything involving fine motor skills, such as writing, my hand shakes a lot. Fortunately, I can type some. Not like I used to, when I typed almost 50 words a minute, but I'm able to hunt and peck keys with my left hand. In spite of, or maybe because of all that I went through after the accident, today I'm an author in a book — this very book you're reading now!

I live in the moment and embrace life fully, because you don't ever know how many days you have left. I encourage you to do the same! My life changed in an instant, and today, I'm a motivator to the unmotivated in life as a motivational speaker and wellness coach! You just have to keep your eye on the ball and your head in the game. That way, no matter what life throws you, you can be prepared to adjust and appreciate as necessary. I have fought long and hard to be where I am today, and my new dream is now to inspire people to change their lives because truly, anything is possible!

Make It Count
Jeff Marconette

"You are already in pain. Why not get a reward for it?"
— Eric Thomas

"No matter how bad things are or how bad things get, I am going to make it." — Les Brown

January 7, 2017 marked 15 years that I have been living since being given a second chance at life. Most people don't get a second chance. When I came out of my 2 ½ month coma, my parents didn't know at first if I would even remember who they were. Nobody knew at first if I would ever be able to walk, talk, or live a normal life.

But I did remember. And I did relearn how to walk and talk. It wasn't easy, and it sometimes felt impossible, but I'm here today as proof that you can do more than you ever thought possible. That's why I celebrate every moment, because I know that they're precious and they matter.

You only have one life. Why not make it count? Regardless of what's happened to you, or whatever setbacks you may have experienced, you have untapped strength and ability within you. In life, it's 10% what happens to you, and 90% how you *react* to what happens to you. Your problems are not the problem — it's your reaction. If I had reacted negatively to what happened to me and taken pity on myself, I wouldn't be where I am today. A defeatist attitude will always lead to defeat.

When people told me that there were things I couldn't do, I responded by proving them wrong. Because I was determined to keep going and never quit, I've been able to share my experience and reach people in a number of ways. My physical therapist also ran the Drive Alive program, a court-appointed program for teens and young adults who have been convicted of things like speeding, DUI, running stop signs, and the like. Drawing from my own experience of being in a traumatic, life-changing accident, I've spoken at the program for over nine years. I wasn't under the influence of drugs or alcohol when my accident happened, but I know all too well how profoundly your life can change in the blink of an eye. Miami Valley Hospital even honored my participation in the Drive Alive program by putting my framed picture on the volunteer wall. The program also hosts alcohol fairs, where I set up my own booth, take pictures, and talk to students.

I was in a driver's education video called "Making the Right Choice," which shows the outcome of driving under the influence, or while texting or being otherwise distracted. So many people have a mindset of "it can't happen to me," but the decisions made in a split second can mean life or death. It's so important that people make the right choices on the road, because there are some actions you can never undo or come back from.

In the 15 years that have passed since the accident, I've overcome immense obstacles to do some pretty great things with my life. My experience in volunteering, sharing my story, and connecting with people is what opened the door to getting into motivational speaking. I first discovered Eric Thomas, one of my favorites, through a friend of mine. It grew from there, and I was listening to and gaining wisdom from different motivational speakers and life coaches. I hope that now, as I share my story, it can help change and save people's lives, minds, and hearts, just as I was influenced by the motivational speakers I listen to.

Today, I'm an international world team member for Herbalife, an Herbalife independent distributor, a motivational speaker, and a health and wellness coach at a local fitness center. My mission is to change the world with a focus on nutrition, a positive mindset, and fitness.

If you're ready to answer the call on your life and overcome your obstacles, there are five steps you must take. They worked for me, and I know that they will work for you. When you do, you can make the rest of your life the best of your life!

1. **Make the decision to be happy, to be successful, and to live a full life.** The first thing you must do is decide what you want, how much you want it, and when you want it to happen. Then, you need to write it down, draw it, or design it. You can do this by journaling or making a dream board. Post your dream board somewhere that you'll see it on a daily basis. Once you get started, don't let anyone stand in your way — including your own self-doubt. The only person who can truly hold you back or

propel you forward is *you.* It's time to become your biggest fan!

2. **Change your mind — change your life.** Fill your mind with useful ideas, and not just ones that take up space. Be mindful of your thoughts, as well as the things you listen to. When you allow fear and negativity to dominate your mindset, it keeps you from growing or moving forward.

   Get a gratitude journal, and start each day by writing down something you're grateful for. This helps you make the shift into a positive mindset, rather than focusing on the negative. You should also do "I am" statements. When you are fearful or falling into an "I can't" mindset, "I am" statements will help you turn it around into something positive. Here are some examples of "I am" statements to get you started:

   - I am responsible for my own life.
   - I am determined to succeed.
   - I am worthy of living my best life.
   - I am able to help myself.
   - I am able to help others.
   - I am better every day.

3. **Erase "I can't" from your vocabulary.** When I was learning to eliminate "I can't" from my thoughts, words, and actions, I would do pushups anywhere and anytime it was said. I did five pushups for every "can't," and I've done them everywhere from the chiropractor's office to

the middle of Wal-Mart! Even if you don't do pushups, you have to find a way to cut negative things and people from your life, because they are holding you back.

4. **Develop strong core values, an undeniable personal philosophy, and a true mission statement.** This goes hand-in-hand with your dream board from step one. You need to know what you're doing and why you're doing it. Remember that if you don't like something in your life, it's up to *you* to change something. You can't keep the same things and people around you while expecting different results. Life doesn't work like that.

5. **Learn to celebrate every moment of your life.** Your life can end in the blink of an eye. Your life can also change drastically in the blink of an eye. People get complacent, but everything can be different when you wake up the next morning. That's why it's so important to stop living in the past or waiting for the future and embrace what's happening here and now!

Your life isn't going to change until you start doing things differently, because you are in control of what happens to you. The past and everything that has happened in it is gone, and it's what you do now and in the future that matters. My purpose in life is to serve others by helping people live their true potential. Whether it's health, wealth, or confidence, I'm driven to help people live the best life they can live and be happy.

I'm grateful to share my story with the world and be an inspiration to other people. If I could choose only one word to describe the message of my life, it would be "gratitude." I'm thankful for every second of every day that I have been given. I was given a second chance at life, and I'm not going to waste it. I'm going to make it count, and so should you!

Jeff Marconette

Jeff Marconette is an international world team member for Herbalife, an Herbalife independent distributor, a motivational speaker, and a health and wellness coach.

Jeff is a highly energetic lover of every moment, and a very loud motivator to the unmotivated in life. At the age of 17, Jeff was in an accident that left him in a coma for 2 ½ months. He suffered a traumatic brain injury as a result of the accident, which means he had to go through the rigorous process of learning how to do basic things, like walking and talking, all over again.

Jeff has been recognized for his volunteer service to programs like Drive Alive and the United States Air Force. In October of 2016, he received the Sharing Your Voice award at the Blackbelt Speakers live training event, held in Stone Mountain, Georgia. Jeff is known for his positive attitude, and is committed to posting encouraging, inspirational content on platforms like Facebook and Instagram to combat the negative mindset of others.

Jeff's chapters in *Live Your Best Life: Answer the Call* are dedicated to his mother, Judith Marconette, who left this earth on October 21, 2016. She was immensely proud and happy to know that Jeff's story would be featured in the book, and her memory lives on through Jeff's commitment to celebrate each moment and live life to the fullest.

If you're ready to stop living in the past, stop waiting on the future, and live your best life right here and now, you can contact Jeff by email at inspiredbyjeff@yahoo.com.

You can also connect with Jeff on social media.

Facebook: https://www.facebook.com/jefijr
Instagram: https://www.instagram.com/jeff_iam24fit/

"Change your mind — change your life." — Garrain Jones

"Shoot for the moon. Even if you miss, you'll land among the stars." — Les Brown

"Things are only impossible until someone does them." — Unknown

There's Always Tomorrow
Dr. Adria E. Luster

"Procrastination is opportunity's assassin." – Victor Kiam

Anyone who knows me personally will tell you that my favorite holiday is Christmas. Growing up in Kansas, we always had a snowy "White Christmas" that was filled with the enjoyment of snowball fights, making snow angels, and sledding. On Christmas Eve, my siblings and I would sit around the television, drinking hot cocoa and eating cookies while watching the 1964 animated production of *Rudolph the Red-Nosed Reindeer*. One of the songs I love from this tale is sung by Rudolph's girlfriend, Clarice. The song, "There's Always Tomorrow," is meant to encourage Rudolph to accept his differences and focus on his attributes. As a child, I thought the music and words were catchy, but I did not realize that the song also sums up how busy adults often view life:

There's always tomorrow,

With so much to do,

And do little time in a day.

Think about it. How many times have you said, *"I'll do it tomorrow! I haven't got time today!"* because you felt you needed to do something more important? Or how many times have you arrived home from work, dropped down on the couch, turned on the T.V. and said, *"Whatever didn't get done will have to wait until tomorrow. I'm gonna watch the game!"* The time we spend being non-productive can never be replaced. Unlike water, energy, or any other resource, time can NEVER be recycled. Each day begins anew. Time can NEVER be replaced. Once a moment has passed, it will never return. Time can NEVER be relived. A picture or video of an event will never the capture the pure essence of the experience. Time is our most valuable resource, and yet, it is not always treated as such.

Edward Young once said, "Procrastination is the thief of time." Of course, we never realize how much time has been stolen from us until we face the possibility that we may not cross off all of the items on our "Bucket List" because Death is knocking at our door. I say this from experience, and I am sharing my story so that I can prevent someone else from waiting until they face the possibility of dying before they decide to make a change in their lives.

Webster's defines the word procrastinate as "To put off intentionally and habitually." The Latin roots of the word can be broken down as follows; "pro" meaning *forward*, and "crastinus" meaning *belonging to tomorrow*. In other words, procrastination means that whatever action we have decided to take, we will forward or delay until tomorrow. Now, we've all had those days where we said, "I'm tired. I'll do the laundry tomorrow." That's human nature. There are times when our bodies need rest or we need to mentally unwind from an exhausting day. If this is an occasional occurrence, it probably won't cause a major disruption in your life. However, when this action becomes habitual, it often leads to consequences that we would prefer to avoid. For example, let's consider what might happen if someone delayed that basket of laundry for many days until the pile became so high that they were out of clean clothes. What consequence might this lead to? Well, there's a chance that it might cause them (and their mother) extreme embarrassment! Think about it — they'd probably start digging through the heap and doing the "sniff test" on garments they think they can reuse without washing. Then, they'd rush out for work the next morning and possibly get into an accident while not wearing clean underwear! Imagine the whispers they'd hear amongst the hospital staff the next day: "He pulled through, even though he was wearing filthy underwear!"

Now, we can laugh at the example above, but some of us have FIGURATIVE baskets of clothes that we need to tend to. Baskets filled with unwritten stories, unsung songs, and unsaid words. Take a moment and consider this — what if tomorrow does not come for you? You can turn on the news each morning and see the name of someone who did not live to see another day. Despite what the children's song says, at some point in life, we will all face the fact that there is NOT always tomorrow. Death is an eventual reality for every mortal being, and unless you're Superman, it's a reality you will have to face at some point. Sometimes, we have to tell ourselves, "Do the laundry!" in both the literal and figurative sense. Life is too short to let "dirty laundry" hold you back. Push through the Tide and Gain a new perspective that will Cheer you up and push you to work on your dreams! (Pun intended.)

What makes me an authority on procrastination? Well, I've let it hold me back many times during my life. I honestly used to joke with my friends that I was the "Queen of Procrastination" because I often put off tasks that I did not want to do, or filled my time doing things that I felt were more significant. As a mother and an educator, there was always something or someone that I felt was more important than me. However, I realized the error of my ways when I faced the possibility that my time on this planet might be severely limited or even end. I felt robbed when I thought about how I hadn't "made my mark" in this world. I was certain that people would attend my memorial and say nice things about me: former students would talk about how I was a caring and dedicated teacher; my children would say I was a loving parent; my husband would speak about my excellent culinary skills. I imagined myself, looking down from above and watching my funeral in anger because no one spoke about the great works of literature that I had written because I had neglected to release all of the stories and poems that I had held inside.

How did I get to this point? **I arrived at this critical destination because of my procrastination!** It snuck up on me like a 'thief in the night' and almost got away with my treasures! In hindsight, I wish that I'd viewed procrastination as the enemy it truly was instead of as an ally. I wish that I had said to myself, as I am recommending you do right now, *"My goals and dreams are valuable and I refuse to let procrastination steal them away from me!"*

In January of 2013, I remember feeling a funny knot in my left breast. I shared my discovery with a friend, and she suggested that I go to the doctor. I delayed actually going to the doctor's office because I had other work duties that I thought were more important. It was the second semester, and I had student testing and graduation to focus on. I teach in an urban district, and my students are those that many consider to be "at-risk" and in need of extreme interventions and support to achieve success. Because I was focusing more on them, I neglected my health and decided to wait to get it checked until the summer. Little did I know that this decision would come back to haunt me. During my summer months, I procrastinated even more and filled my days with vacations and shopping trips during May and June. When I finally and reluctantly went at the end of July, (and only because the friend that I had confided in urged me to) it was one week before the new school year was about to begin. Imagine my surprise when the doctor told me that the 'knot' I disregarded as a minor issue was actually a tumor and that further tests were needed.

A few weeks later, I was diagnosed with cancer. Once I received the news, I was not sure of how advanced it was and whether I would live or die. I was only told that the tumor was malignant and that even further tests would be needed. I thought to myself, *"If only I'd checked on this in January, maybe it might not have come to this point. There's a chance that it may have spread throughout my system and I could have stopped it!"*

I thought about my unfinished goals and dreams. Sure, I'd accomplished a lot — numerous degrees, including a doctorate, a successful career as an educator, and a loving and stable marriage. However, I wanted to achieve so much more! I had always wanted to be a writer, and I worried that I would leave earth without the opportunity to tell my story. Maya Angelou once said, "There is no greater agony than bearing an untold story inside you." It had been my lifelong dream to be an author, and I had many stories that I wanted to share with the world.

Not knowing if you will live or die and having to wait in excess of two weeks for a prognosis is pure torture. Having only had basic medical tests for pregnancy and other minor situations, I was of the mindset that it would be as simple as dropping my blood on a stick and waiting five minutes for it to change color. I was definitely wrong. Because everyone's cancer is different, a person's entire body chemistry has to be examined before a prognosis can be given. Once I was told that I had cancer, my first question was, "Will I die?" Hearing the doctor say, "Well, we will have to do some testing before we can answer that" places you on an emotional edge. I often wondered why people who faced grave illnesses refused to tell their loved ones. Having been in that situation, I now understand why. I personally decided not to tell anyone in my family about my diagnosis until I had a full prognosis. I remember screening calls from my mother and sisters because I was scared that if they heard my voice, they'd be able to tell that something was wrong. I didn't want anyone to worry about me, especially when I didn't have any answers to give them.

When I received my formal diagnosis, I felt even sadder when I reflected on all of the moments I'd wasted doing idle tasks instead of pursuing my dreams. A biopsy of my tumor revealed that I suffered from an aggressive form of stage II breast cancer, and that my tumor was growing so rapidly that there was a strong likelihood that it would spread. When I received the news, I reflected on the "what if's" of my situation — **What if** I had visited a doctor in January instead of putting it off until the summer in order to suit someone else's needs? **What if** I had achieved more of the goals I had set for myself instead of facing the reality that my life path might abruptly end? Les Brown calls the graveyard the richest place on earth because it holds the books that were never written because someone was too afraid to take the first step. **What if** my stories died with me in my grave?

Once I had begun treatment, I shared my diagnosis with a few close friends, including Dr. Ruben West. He asked me, "If you were to leave, what is the one thing you wish that you had taken the time to do?" I was shocked at first, because I had only discussed my situation with a few people and he was the first person to provide an alternate viewpoint. Everyone else tried to give me the usual comforting words, or question whether my financial affairs were in order. Dr. West, who has been like a brother to me since we were kids, was the first person to question me about my actual life's purpose. I told him the honest truth.

"I know this may sound crazy, but I have ALWAYS wanted to be an author. Even when I was young, I used to write stories for my friends. I would love to see my name printed on a book." Mind you, at the time of this conversation, I've already had the tumor removed and completed my first few sessions of chemo. I was completely bald, feeling about 40 years older, extremely depressed, and on medical leave from work.

He responded to me as if I was a five year old and the solution was plain and simple: "So, why don't you write your book right now? Are you planning to die?"

I was speechless. I sarcastically thought to myself, *"No, I wasn't planning to die. I mean, I hadn't actually penciled this cancer vacation in on my calendar. Time off from work is great, but when it's accompanied by doctor's visits every other day, well..."*

He laughed and responded as if he were reading my mind. "There's an old saying that goes, *'If you want to make God laugh, tell Him your plans.'* Life happens. The question is, how are you going to respond to it?"

Still speechless, I must admit that I "got into my feelings" and felt a little indignant at the lack of sympathy that I was receiving from my "brother." He continued by telling me, "It's never too late to follow your dreams. Sometimes we face a setback so that we can make a comeback."

After we ended our conversation, I pondered on what Dr. West had said to me. The answer really was simple, and the choice was up to me. Maybe this was a sign from God that I needed to share my gift. There's an old saying that I'll cleanly paraphrase: "Sometimes it comes down to two choices, we can either (release ourselves) or get off the pot." I decided that I was going to get off my pity pot and take action. Procrastination had led me down this path, so I knew that I couldn't count on it to get me back on track.

As I said before, **I had arrived at this critical destination because of my procrastination**. I knew that I couldn't use the same strategies to get myself out of this situation. When time is of the essence, we tend to act quickly. However, when you're trying to achieve a goal while facing a major obstacle in your life, the road is even rougher and you often reflect on how much easier it would have been if you'd pursued it when things were smoother. But time, our most valuable resource, cannot be recycled, replaced, or relived.

Imagine that you are driving your car in rush hour traffic. You're approaching a stoplight, and your left back wheel goes flat. You can still move, so you tell yourself that you'll pull over into the parking lot at the corner. As you approach the light, your front left wheel falls off. You try not to panic, and say to yourself, "I'm going to make this sharp right turn on my two right wheels and I'll be okay." You know that a car can't adequately run on two wheels, but you've seen Wiley Coyote do this trick a few times in some of the cartoons you watched when you were a kid, so you think it's a possibility. Picture yourself at this moment and visualize the emotions that you would feel. You're tightly gripping the steering wheel. There's a level of panic that sits in the pit of your gut that is fueled by a strong rush of adrenaline-induced determination. You figure that you might as well try it, because you really don't have any other options. And who's to say that it can't be done? This feeling of panic and uncertainty that is fueled by the will to survive is a lot like how it feels when you are fighting for your life. All of us have or will face situations such as this in our lifetimes. Sometimes, we are confronted with obstacles that are so great that all we have to get us through is our will to survive.

My cancer diagnosis created a major disruption in my daily life and what I considered to be "normal" will never be a reality for me again. Prior to beginning treatment, I visited so many specialists and had so many tests conducted that I was literally at a medical facility every day for about two weeks. The question, "Will I live?" hung over me like a stormy raincloud for the first few weeks because I did not know the extent of my illness. *Was it stage IV? Had it ravaged my body to the extent that it was incurable?* I had to eventually take a leave of absence from work because the numerous appointments made it impossible to fulfill my duties. After I received a few answers *("It's stage II, but it's VERY aggressive! We rarely see cases like this!")* my life felt like I was driving on a flat tire. I was moving along, but I couldn't go fast and I could suffer a blow-out at any time. I honestly realized that there was a strong possibility that my tomorrow might never come.

This diagnosis also helped me understand that not only does it cost a lot of money to be sick, but people really DON'T CARE about your excuses or your situation because they have their own lives to live. There are so many expenses that we don't consider when we are healthy, such as the gas needed for multiple doctor and specialist visits that are sometimes 30-40 miles from your home, or the countless meals that you must eat from restaurants because you are too weak or ill to cook. And finally, the cost of prescription co-pays, even WITH insurance coverage. I remember one incident when I was being administered chemotherapy and I received a phone call from a bill collector that was trying to get me to pay $300 on a $100,000 surgery bill. I tried to explain to the collector that I was unable to schedule a payment because I was still off work and receiving treatment. The collector continued with her script, and the nurse, who was beside me setting up my IV, overheard her. Mind you, we are in a large room that is full of about 20 other individuals receiving treatment. The nurse, who was an older lady, authoritatively asked me, "Is that who I think it is?" I nodded my head affirmatively. She then responded loud enough for the caller to hear, "Hey! She's getting chemo RIGHT NOW!" The caller continued speaking and the nurse heard her. She began to yell, even louder, "Give me the phone! Give me the goddamn phone!" The other patients in the background cheered loudly, and the caller quieted down before timidly saying, "Mrs. Luster, I think I will call you back at a better time." As I hung up the phone, I was amazed at the callousness of the medical billing process. True, I'd heard stories about the fierceness of creditors, and even experienced a few back in the day, but credit card bills are created through purposeful actions. Medical bills are not. I felt that the difference should garner a slight bit of sympathy, but when I look at the situation from a practical standpoint, I must admit that I understand. The payment of my bill would be split among countless entities and individuals, including the multiple doctors and specialists, the anesthesiologist, nurses, and even the debt collector. All of them had their lives to live and their own bills that needed to be paid with MY money. My excuses would not put money in their pockets and just like I needed my income, they also needed theirs. The reality is that in life, no one really wants to hear your excuses; they just want to know how you're going to fix the problem.

On a physical level, cancer treatments cause major changes to a person's appearance. This can lead to serious damage to one's self-esteem. For example, I'd always had long, thick hair that flowed down my back. When I was young, people often would mistakenly think it was a weave. Losing it all to the point where my head was so clean that it shined stubble-free like Michael Jordan's was a drastic change for me. I had to endure the triple-threat of treatments — surgery (which left scars), chemotherapy (which left me bald and weak), and radiation (which caused extreme exhaustion and excruciating burns). It was hard for me to focus on achieving my life's goals with so many changes taking place. However, I knew that unlike before, I might not have a second chance and I had no time to waste by procrastinating.

On a personal level, I realized how life-altering illnesses can affect relationships. I always wondered why some divorces occurred after a person had fought a battle with a serious illness. The personal, physical, financial, and emotional changes can cause some weakened relationships to break apart. Thankfully, I felt that this ordeal strengthened my marriage. My vulnerability caused me to lean on my husband more, both emotionally and physically, and he didn't let me down. (A guy that'll wipe your forehead with a cold towel when you're sick, wipe your back when you're sweating, and even wipe your... well, that's a pretty good guy in my book!) This made me realize that he truly cared for me. Plus, he'd seen me at my worse and still told me I was beautiful. (Except for that time I tried to camouflage my bald head with a gangster-style fedora hat. He was honest enough to tell me I looked stupid!)

Cancer is difficult to deal with because it causes such a major disruption in all aspects of your life. Also, while a person may be receiving treatment and facing a healthy recovery, there is still the constant threat to their health due to their compromised immune system. For example, many people recovering from cancer often die from immune-related illnesses, such as pneumonia, something that most healthy individuals don't succumb to.

Cancer is a serious obstacle, yet the facets of its impact can be the same in similarly life-altering scenarios, such as the death of a loved one, a divorce, a loss of employment, or being given the task of caring for a loved one that is dealing with an illness, such as Alzheimer's. At some point, we will all face situations when we can't throw in the towel. However, the battles we fight ALONE give us our greatest lessons. Michael Jordan, who many consider to be the greatest athlete of all time, has said, "There is no 'I' in team, but there is in WIN." One thing that I learned is that some battles might seem physical, but they are really a battle of the mind. Keeping the mind focused on positive things helps the body recover. By focusing so much on my goal of being a published author, I shifted my thoughts away from many of the negative things taking place. I thought about a quote I once heard — *"Adopting the right attitude can change a negative situation into a positive one."*

During this period, I gradually designed five basic rules that I would follow in order to maintain my sanity as well as my independence. After becoming slightly depressed after the numerous tests and countless doctor's visits, I realized that the emotional aspect had the potential to do more damage than the physical. I reflected on something I'd once heard the Rev. T. D. Jakes say: *"For every struggle in your life, there is a strategy."* I decided to strategize my situation and come up with a game plan, and so at this point, I drafted my first rule.

Rule Number One was that I had to leave my house EVERY DAY and go SOMEWHERE. I refused to stay in the bed because I feared that it would cause further depression. One of my father-in-law's mantras is, "The bed will kill you." (This is a man who acts and looks 20 years younger than he is, that rises with the sun and takes a walk outside each and every day, so I consider him a reliable source.) During chemotherapy, I was also administered a drug called Nuelasta that uses the bone marrow to activate the white blood cells and increase immunity. One of the side effects is extreme bone and joint pain that limits mobility. On some days, I would struggle to drive to the Dollar Tree, located less than a mile from my house, get out of my car, and walk around. Each step would cause excruciating pain, similar to how it feels when you hit your funny bone. I walked at the pace of an 80-year-old woman, step by painful step. On some days, it would take me an hour to walk around the store, a trip I could normally do in ten minutes. However, I stuck with my plan. I visited there so frequently that I eventually made friends with the staff and they would comment on my progress and recovery. To this day, I still see and speak to many of these people when I shop there on occasion.

Rule Number Two was that I would leave chemo treatment and visit the gym each week. I could only walk on the treadmill, and sometimes at a pace of 1.5 miles an hour at a zero incline, but I went. My nurses would encourage me and tell me that by doing this, I was actually helping myself because I caused the treatment to flush through my system faster. When I'd arrive for treatment in my gym gear, they'd make positive remarks and say things like, "Going to the gym again? You go, girl!"

Rule Number Three was that I cooked at home as often as I could. This provided me with a task to do each day and a purpose for getting out of bed. Even on a day of chemo, when I felt fatigued, I would bake a chicken and cook a pot of rice. My poor husband endured the same meal on every chemo day and never complained. I thought he was fine with it until I decided to change it up and add some barbeque sauce to the chicken and fix macaroni and cheese instead of rice on a day that I felt slightly better than normal. When he sat down that evening he said, "Alright! Something else besides plain baked chicken." I could only roll my eyes at him and laugh!

Rule Number Four required me to write positive statements or mantras on my mirror and repeat them each morning. Sometimes, the quotes were from famous people, such as "Tough times never last, but tough people do." Other times, the quotes were just things I heard from people in my life or from fictional characters in stories. After my first surgery, my mother-in-law came to visit. Before she left she hugged me and said, "Alright, girl. You're strong. You can fight this. Be a soldier." Before going to bed, I wrote that mantra on my mirror. *BE A SOLDIER.*

That night, I dreamed of my husband's great aunt, Minnie Mae. She was such a loving person, and she had passed recently from a heart-related illness. She'd once made me laugh because she referred to her cancer treatment as "chemistry" instead of chemotherapy. She had lived in Albany, Georgia, the hometown of my husband's family, and we would visit her a few times each year. On one occasion, I was visiting with her in her home and she was cooking for me. (She was a GREAT cook!) She'd expressed how she hated her short hair and said, "I'm glad I'm finished with that chemistry. My hair is finally growing back." I'd told her that I didn't know she had undergone chemo and she said, "Yes, Honey. That cancer ain't gonna get me." She'd faced her battle so bravely, and I honestly think her positive attitude helped her make it through. I hadn't begun chemo yet, and I wondered if I would have the same attitude that she had. When I awoke from my dream, I felt that Minnie Mae was giving me a message of hope and offering me the chance to have a POSITIVE outlook on my situation. Once I began chemotherapy, I learned more about the disease and how each person's treatment was tailored specifically for their body. I laughed when I realized that she was actually using the correct term! I decided to alter my view of the medicine and instead of viewing it negatively, see it as a special concoction made for my individual chemistry. After my first chemotherapy session, I wrote the word CHEMISTRY on my mirror.

The next week, I reread the classic novel, *A Tree Grows in Brooklyn.* The story is set at beginning of the 19th century. At the onset of the book, the main character's mother is described as strong and resilient. *"Katie had a fierce desire for survival which made her a fighter."* Throughout the story, Katie continues to get knocked down in life (she suffers the shame of an alcoholic husband, she works to support her family, she becomes a widow) and yet, she continues to get back up and keep fighting. That evening, I wrote the following on my mirror: I AM KATIE NOLAN. While Katie is a fictional character, I felt a kinship with her situation because I also had a fierce desire to survive so that I could fulfill the goals and dreams that I wanted to achieve. Sometimes, we have to find someone to identify with in order to gain the encouragement and inspiration we need, whether it's a famous person, fictional character, or family member.

On another occasion, I read a poem by Maya Angelou for inspiration. It was during a difficult period when I felt down because by now, most of the hair had left my body and I did not feel beautiful. I thought about her poem, "Phenomenal Woman," and how beauty comes from the inside of a person. I considered the fact that there were countless examples of physically attractive women on reality television shows who acted so hateful and mean that their beauty appeared to diminish every time the camera focused on them. I thought of the India Arie song, "I Am Not My Hair," in which she sings about a woman who also faced this dilemma by finding pride in her inner beauty. I recalled meeting Ms. Arie a couple of years earlier in a public place, and how impressed I was at her politeness and gracious character, which personified the character she sang about. I stared at my reflection, and wrote these two phrases on the mirror: PHENOMENAL WOMAN and I AM NOT MY HAIR. After a while, my mirror was covered with positive words that I would use for encouragement. In fact, I began to list so many that it became harder and harder to see my reflection. Each morning, I wasn't confronted with the image of my illness, but I was bombarded with **positive** words and images that helped me see past what I looked like on the outside and helped me forget about the negative. (I think my husband began to think I was "going off the deep end" because he asked me when I was going to clean the mirror. I firmly told him that he had his OWN mirror and sink and to please leave my space alone. He got the message and NEVER asked again.) It sounds funny, but there's a lesson here: there are times when we have to encourage ourselves so that we can drown out the negativity in our lives. It doesn't matter how you do it — you might use post-it notes, poems, motivational speeches, or songs, but whatever it takes, just find a way to make it happen.

Finally, **Rule Number Five** required me to maintain

my emotional health by pursuing my dream and writing my book during chemotherapy treatments. I developed this rule after my life-altering discussion with Dr. West, and it was probably the rule that had the greatest impact on both my physical and mental health.

Many people do not know this, but for some people such as myself, the process of undergoing chemotherapy can take 5-7 hours. At first, I would sit in the large room and watch television or nap like everyone else. If you've never seen a chemo treatment room, I'll describe it for you. Imagine a room with comfortable La-Z-Boy chairs all around the wall. In the middle of the room, there are about four televisions posted, one in each direction, so that they can be viewed from any area. Last, there's a drink station that serves hot K-Cup beverages and cold sodas and juices. There is also an area with healthy snacks and crackers. Sounds like a pretty cool place, right? I mean, if the beverage station served beer, it would be the ideal "Man Cave" or media room. Now, add to this about 4 nurses, and place an IV next to each chair. Each person is hooked to a medicinal drip, and most people are also covered in a blanket. Some people also have oxygen tanks or walkers next to their chairs. Now it doesn't sound so appealing, huh?

The average person would probably picture a group of old people meeting up in this room. And the average person would be dead wrong. At 44, I was one of the "older" people present. There was a teenager who was still in high school. There was also a young pregnant woman. There was an old white man that looked like he could be a member of the cast of Duck Dynasty. There was a short Asian man who reminded me of the owner of my favorite Chinese restaurant. Every age and race was represented. People that would normally be reluctant to approach me due to societal constraints would hold lengthy conversations with me, discussing medications, procedures, and strategies for dealing with our common ailment. In a strange way, this sickness had the ability to breakdown all racial and societal barriers. The irony that cancer lacked prejudice was unsettling.

Because chemotherapy is scheduled, the same patients are present at basically the same time each week. After a few sessions, you might begin to address each other by name, or at least say "hello" or give a head nod when you see them. Now, here's the hard part of this ordeal and why I think many people give up: once you become accustomed to seeing someone regularly, you also miss them when they are gone. Sometimes, I'd overhear someone say, "You know, Joe got pneumonia. He's at Grady." Or one of the nurses might say, "Mr. Chang can't come in any more. He's in a hospice." Watching this around me started to dampen my spirits. I started to dread going to my appointment for fear that someone else might not be there.

I decided to use this time to write because it allowed me to "zone out" and gain a positive focus. I would lug my laptop and plug it in next to my IV. Instead of watching television, I would put on my headphones and listen to music. I was polite, and I would nod to everyone, but I wanted to shift my focus to maintain my sanity. John Milton said that

"A good book is the precious lifeblood of a master spirit." When I would get into the characters, I would sometimes feel as if I was transformed from my physical setting into a more desirable environment.

Due to God's divine intervention, I also had the physical presence of my husband to lean on. In hindsight, I honestly think that nothing happens by chance because he had been laid off and was seeking employment when I learned of my diagnosis. After a few weeks of treatment, I realized the toll that it was taking on me both emotionally and physically, and I asked him to refrain from seeking another full-time position so that he could serve as my caretaker. He agreed. He maintained a part-time job that was close to home so that he could check on me. However, I rarely called on him because the knowledge that he was close by provided me with a strong sense of security. I also wanted the opportunity to spend more time with him, if by chance I did not recover. I knew that our time together was precious, and I dared not waste it. Now that I recognized the error of my ways, I vowed to change. As someone once said, "Some of life's best lessons are learned at the worst times."

Live for Today!
Dr. Adria E. Luster

"Live today! Do not allow your spirit to be softened of your happiness to be limited by a day you cannot have back or a day that does not yet exist." — Steve Maraboli

The rules that I established for myself during my ordeal developed organically because of my experience. Although I didn't realize it at the time, there was a "method to my madness" and each rule was essential to my journey. Had I subtracted one or neglected to develop one of them, my outcome might have been different. I still live by these rules, even though they might not encompass the same activities. Also, I am now able to verbalize them more concisely as a series of steps that I hope can help someone else answer the call on their life.

Step 1. Establish and Maintain a Positive Routine
Mike Murdock said that "The secret to our futures is hidden in our daily routines." In other words, sometimes we must change our routine to reach the goals we want. This change may require us to STOP doing some things and BEGIN doing others. Oftentimes, our personal routine might be out of the norm, because we are trying to "break out" from the pack and embark on a different path.

Sometimes, others might not understand our routine, but WE know what's best for us. I can't tell you how many friends and loved ones advised me to "take it easy" and remain at home and in bed. But I knew that by requiring myself to get out and complete daily tasks, my routine forced me to address my physical and emotional development. Sometimes I would endure gut-wrenching pain as I got out of bed. However, I can honestly say that I NEVER had a day in bed. NEVER. On the morning after my first surgery, my husband cooked me some scrambled eggs. In almost 20 years of marriage, this was his second time cooking for me. And his LAST. He told me they were eggs. But they resembled little dusty yellow pebbles. I struggled to swallow them, and by that evening I had a chicken in the oven. I remember that I was so weak that he had to open the oven for me and place the pan inside. The doctor had advised me to get some rest because I had undergone a major surgery less than 24 hours prior. Yet by moving my tired and aching body, I began to bounce back a lot quicker. Mentally, I would will myself to get up each day and complete my routine because it gave me something to look forward to.

We all have routines we complete EACH and EVERY day without fail. Before leaving the house each morning, we all wash our bodies, brush our teeth, and dress ourselves. Many of us extend the routine even farther by making sure we have a hot cup of coffee. Jerry Seinfeld once joked, "We didn't get a good night's sleep, we're a little depressed. Coffee solves all these problems in one delightful little cup!" Now imagine if you neglected to complete one of these tasks. I'm sure that everyone at the office would have something to say, even if they said it behind your back, if you decided not to wash your body or brush your teeth. And I'm sure many of us would not arrive in a positive mood if we hadn't had our cup of coffee or tea. (I know I wouldn't!)

Sean Covey said, "Our habits will either make us or break us. We become what we repeatedly do." Sometimes, we must recognize our bad or non-productive habits and alter them so that they help us achieve our goals. Brushing your teeth each morning is not only a positive routine; it's a productive habit because it helps you maintain good health. When we decide to answer the call on our lives, we sometimes have to add new habits to our daily routine, as well as discard old ones that are non-productive. There was a researcher in the 1950s who theorized that it took 21 days to form a new habit. A recent study by Phillippa Lally suggests that while 21 days might work for some people, it actually takes about 2 ½ months, or 66 days, for the majority of people to develop a new habit. In other words, if you attempt to make a change and you don't feel like you've successfully mastered it in 21 days, it's okay. Keep trying. You are on track and developing at the rate of most people.

Think back to when you were a kid. I'm sure your mother had to remind you to wash your face or brush your teeth a few times. But eventually, you got it. What if she'd said, "You'll never get it. Let's just give up on this toothbrushing habit." Wow. Think of how different your life, as well as your smile, might be. In the same token, we shouldn't be so hard on ourselves when we still struggle with a change after 21 days and throw in the towel. Keep pushing, keep trying. Brian Tracy said that "Successful people are simply those with successful habits." As you develop each positive habit, you are one step closer to success.

Step 2. Make Yourself a Priority

Maya Angelou stated that it's hard to trust a person that loves you more than they love themselves. In other words, self-love must happen first before we can truly love others. This was something that I'd previously had trouble doing without feeling some level of guilt (and I still struggle with this), but this was also the reason that I **arrived at my critical destination due to procrastination.** Taking care of my own body had been put on the back burner. And I now had scars and a bald head to show for it. By choosing to exercise, I was learning to focus on ME. I was teaching myself that despite the circumstances, I CAME FIRST. Of course, exercise is just one thing that you can do for yourself. You might choose to take a walk in the park. Or treat yourself to a drink from Starbucks. Or take a warm bath while reading a book with the door locked so the kids won't interrupt you.

Many times, women, especially mothers, have a hard time caring for themselves because it seems selfish. I remember when my children were little and I'd go in the bathroom and close the door, only to be interrupted by, "Mom, how much longer are you going to be in there?" Or to submerge myself in a relaxing bubble bath only to be interrupted by them saying, "If we sit on this side of the door, can we still talk to you?" Seriously, I am not making this up. If you don't believe me, ask a mother that you know, or even your own, and they will verify that getting "alone time" is about as easy as negotiating World Peace. However, preserving your mental and physical well-being is one of the greatest gifts you can give to your loved ones. It may involve you setting some boundaries or altering your routine so that you can avoid interference. Very few children will wake up at 5:00 a.m. demanding breakfast. And if they do, leave a Pop-Tart and a glass of milk on the counter to tide them over until you return from your morning jog. I have a co-worker who has a toddler. She visits the gym at 5 each morning, returns at 6, takes her shower, dresses, and then gets him up at 6:30. As someone who has no children at home and still rolls over and hits the snooze button sometimes, I have to admit that I felt quite shamed when she explained the effort she took to maintain her health. But she shared with me that she'd once battled a serious illness and decided to make her physical well-being a top priority because she now had a child to rear. Think about your family. Are they important enough for you to do what's best for them? We like to say that our family is important, and that's why we put them first. But if they are really important, we'll put ourselves first. They might whine, but that is simply because you are asking them to adjust to a change. However, I'm sure that they'd rather give up one hour a day with you instead of suffering without you for through the rest of their lives.

This rule also helps you establish and maintain boundaries that will prove to be valuable to you, as well as to your children's emotional and social development. If your children know that Mommy's bubble bath is at 7:00, they will eventually find something else to do until 8:00. If you don't believe me, give them a tablet or an iPhone and see if they can't find a way to occupy themselves for 60 minutes. If your friends call at 7:00 and you're in your regular Zumba class, ignore the call. Eventually, they will stop calling at that time or they might even decide to join you. Good habits are contagious!

Step 3. Feed Yourself Positivity

Have you ever watched a scary movie before bed and then been so uptight that you had to watch something else to calm down so that you can go to sleep? Your mind races because it has been fed so many negative and scary images that your body won't relax. Do you see the mind/body connection? The great Les Brown says that sometimes, we have to "inoculate ourselves with positive words and images." In other words, when you feed your mind nutritious food, it becomes stronger. Let me give you an example. I live in Atlanta, Georgia, and the traffic here is horrendous! My average morning commute to work takes 90 minutes. However, I spend my time listening to motivational speeches and empowering literature. I have found that it not only helps the ride seem faster, but it also helps me arrive at work each day with a positive attitude. As my mind becomes stronger, I find that I can remain calm in situations that might have unnerved me in the past. I also find that the negative inner-dialogue or "voices in my head" don't creep up as much, because I have an overload of affirmations and mantras.

Back when my husband thought I was going "off the deep end" (and maybe I was!) by covering my mirror with encouraging words and phrases, I was actually feeding myself large doses of positivity to combat the negativity I was experiencing. Now, I don't advise anyone to cover their mirror and then show up to work with a piece of spinach in their teeth and a dirty face because they can't see their reflection, but I am suggesting that you do what works for you. Read positive and uplifting literature. View motivational programs. Memorize affirmations and phrases that you can repeat to yourself to combat those negative voices in your head or from others.

Step 4. Work on Your Dream Each and Every Day

There's an old African saying that asks, "How do you eat an elephant? One bite at a time." I remember when I was near the end of my doctoral program and most of my classmates and I began to feel burned out. One of my favorite professors, Dr. Olivia Boggs, placed a picture of an elephant on the board and asked the class this same question. We all laughed, because the concept seemed so simple, yet a few moments before we had all felt discouraged because we were looking at the entire task instead of breaking it down piece by piece.

My life's dream was to become an author. I didn't write all 300 pages of my novel, *Coconut Cake,* in one sitting, but instead wrote a few pages each day. In addition to writing, I also read a lot of literature from my favorite writers as part of my research of their particular styles to help me develop. For some of us, this rule might work best if it is executed along with Step 1 (**Establish and Maintain a Positive Routine**). For example, if begin your day with a cup of coffee, it might be better if you grab your tablet or laptop and write a few pages while you sip your beverage. (My friend, Roz Linder, is now a best-selling author and professional educational trainer. One way she became successful was by following this rule and writing a specific number of pages each day during her daily visit to

Starbucks.) If your dream is to become a culinary chef and you cook dinner every evening, why not choose 1 or 2 nights a week to create new recipes? If you'd love to be a performer, why not get on stage during open-mic night or during karaoke when you hang out each week with your friends?

It's so easy in life to get bogged down with the pressure and demands we sometimes face. During these periods, it is often difficult to work on our dreams. There's an old 90's movie called *Player's Club* that deals with the stress of life from working in a gentleman's club. One of the mantras that the main character, Diamond, repeats throughout the movie is, "Make the money, but don't let the money make you." Now, if you haven't seen the movie, it is an urban film that was written by Ice Cube and it gets rather gritty at times, but it does deliver a powerful message: if your current job or career field is not your true dream, don't allow it to take over all aspects of your life. View it for what it is — money. Sure, you might like your coworkers, or even enjoy what you do. Not everyone is employed at a dead-end job. But if you were told that you only had three years to live, would you keep working there? Or would you decide to answer the call and pursue a dream you've held off because you thought you had more time? If you can't honestly say that you'd stay at your current job, then it is really only a means for you to earn money. We all need money to pay bills, feed our children, and keep a roof over our heads — it is a necessity in this world. However, we should never let it overshadow the dreams and goals we have that provide us with the passion and fulfillment that makes our lives meaningful.

Now, I'm not suggesting that you quit your job and focus solely on your dream. That is a decision that only you can make. However, you can consider the option of working for money while working on your dream simultaneously. In other words, spend at least one hour each day focusing solely on your dream. This may require you to get up one hour earlier, or go to bed one hour later. If you can't find the peace to focus at home, stop off at the local bookstore or mall with your laptop or notebook and jot down ideas. Make it a habit that you do each day.

Finding time for yourself can be difficult, especially if you have a family or loved ones that demand your time. I suggest that you involve them and allow them to work on the process with you. You might be fearful, and want to keep it private. The late, great Erma Bombeck once said, "It takes a lot of courage to show your dreams to someone else." However, if we involve them, we also allow them to share in our accomplishments. And keep in mind, if your dream is financially successful, they WILL want to share the benefits! I remember when I was completing my dissertation — I had two teenage children, and I'd sometimes arrive home, prepared to do some homework, until I'd walk in and hear, "Ma, what's for dinner?" Really?? And I hate to admit it, but I'd actually put my laptop or books down, go into the kitchen, and begin cooking. Now, some of you might be disciplined enough to cook a meal, eat, get full, and then get to work. Sorry, but I'm not one of those people. So, as a result, my classwork was neglected. After this happened a few times, I decided to hatch a plan. One day, I called my kids to the table and we had a Family Forum. They knew that I was pursuing my degree, but as high school students, they really did not understand the level of commitment and concentration required to work a full-time job AND earn a PhD. My oldest daughter, the cook and caretaker of the siblings, was away at college, so I was unable to depend on her for support. And at that moment, I realized how much she assisted with maintaining the household. But since she was not here, I asked them both, "If you had to cook a meal for the family to eat, every week, what could you cook?" They thought about it, and my son named the three things he could cook pretty decently besides Hot Pockets that he knew everyone would eat — tacos, fried chicken, and frozen pizza. My youngest daughter took her turn and named the three things she could cook — baked chicken, hamburgers, and sloppy joes. "Okay," I told them, "here's what we're gonna do. Each of you are going to cook dinner one day a week. I don't care what it is, but it will be one of the items you named. When I come home, no one's gonna ask me what's for dinner because YOU will be cooking. Deal?" We all shook hands and agreed that this option worked best, because it allowed me to complete my assignments without interruption at least twice a week. It wasn't a perfect system, and I occasionally got a knock on the door with questions such as, "How much seasoning salt should I use?" but overall, I was out of the loop and free to pursue my dream of earning my doctorate. When I graduated, I remember seeing their faces beaming with pride because they'd helped me achieve this goal. The next week, I remember my youngest daughter saying, "Mom, can you PLEASE cook every day this week? We miss your cooking!" I was so touched, until she added, "Plus, we're tired of having to eat the same things every Tuesday and Thursday night!"

When I was working on my degree, I knew how important it was to work on my dream each and every day. There were times when I would find a well-lighted parking lot and sit in my car with my laptop for about an hour before going home. Sometimes, it would be the Target just around the corner. Why did I do this? Because if your family's anything like mine, as soon as you enter the door you are often bombarded with "Mama, may I…?" or "Lemme tell you what happened today…" or something else. And it's understandable. We love our family, and we teach each other to interact socially. That's how we develop and maintain our tight bonds. I wasn't trying to avoid this bonding time, just delaying it for an hour or so. I knew that my positive routine would help me achieve my goal and that I didn't need to feel bad about putting myself first so that things would happen for me. There's nothing wrong with that, and there's no reason to feel guilty when you realize that adjustments have to be made in order to answer the call on your life.

Recognizing Your Calling

The late John Glenn once said that "The happiest people are those who call upon the greatest number of their God-given talents and capabilities." We all have talents, and some of us are lucky enough to work in jobs and careers that allow us to use them. However, take a moment and ask yourself: "Am I using ALL of my talents?" You might be a great physician, but you also can use those gifted hands to paint wonderful masterpieces. However, no one has seen them because you are not using ALL of your talents. Or maybe you are a wonderful cosmetologist who can make any woman look glamorous with a new hairstyle, but you also can create beautiful designer clothing that could stand out on any runway. However, no one knows this because you are not using ALL of your talents. I used to be just like you. Fortunately, I worked in a profession that allowed me to use some of my talents, but I was not using ALL of them. Part of the reason was that it took me quite a few years to recognize my calling. And I regret to say that it took me even longer to decide to answer it.

As I've stated before, I often let procrastination and fear hold me back from reaching my true potential. However, early on, I recognized that I was a teacher by trade, and a pretty good one. I've always taught in the inner-city, and I've always been successful with reaching the most difficult kids. Why? I think it is because I strongly identify with them. I was once a student considered "at-risk" and the one everyone spoke negatively of and said wouldn't amount to much of anything. Now, I didn't hear this in the home, but amongst neighbors and relatives and acquaintances at church I'd hear the whispers. I still cringe when I recall some of the hurtful things that were said about me and my family. Why say it for me to hear when I am not responsible for what happened and/or too young to change the situation? Yet, someone once said that we have to turn our "bitterness into better-ness." I recognized that my experiences taught me that words have the ability to both hurt and uplift. As a result, I often used my classroom as a setting to encourage students who had been hurt and belittled by instilling a pride in them that they might not have arrived with. I can recall an experience from when I taught at the middle school level that illustrates how changing a negative into a positive can affect a person's entire outlook on life.

If you've never visited a classroom in Atlanta's inner city, you might not know that most of our African-American male students are usually characterized as "disruptive" or in need of special education services. Some of them are indeed troubled, and I could write a book on the children I've taught that have experienced more hardship and pain before their teen years than the average adult. (Hmmm... maybe I will write that book!) However, many of them are lacking love and compassion and act-out in order to receive attention. One year, I had a 7th grade class comprised of about 70% males. All of my students were African-American, and my classroom represented the varying hues of our race. Now, let me explain something about the culture of the South. It is not something I am proud of, and having come from the Midwest, it was something that took some getting used to. Due to our nation's horrid history, there is still the mindset among some African-Americans that being darker is a negative trait. This concept of intra-racism often leads to children developing poor self-esteem due to their physical characteristics. And we all know that unless you have the wealth of Lil Kim or Sammy Sosa, your complexion is one thing you cannot change. (As a parent of children from all hues of the color spectrum, I personally take offense at this practice and I express an extreme intolerance of it.)

One day, a fair-complexioned female student made a

remark about a darker-complexioned male. I don't want to place her exact words here, because it was such an ugly, derogatory statement that referred to his hue. It was obvious that his feelings were hurt, and I could see the situation was about to get out of control. I looked around the room and noticed that most of my boys were indeed Hershey bar colored or a darker tone, and the tension began to rise like heat off the pavement. I called the young man over to my desk. He was a smart and handsome, and I remembered that while his folder said that he was gifted, he was not placed with the higher-performing team, but was instead in my class of students that needed support. I whispered to him, "Sweetheart, don't let her upset you. There's nothing wrong with being dark. You are a very handsome young man." He looked at me, his back to the class, and to this day I will never forget how my heart ached as I watched the tears of pain slowly fall on his cheeks. He turned and tried to hide them from his classmates. I struggled to remain composed. At that moment, I wanted to lose all elements of my professionalism and embrace him in a big, motherly hug, but I knew that would be frowned upon in this open forum. I called him over to the back of my desk so that his classmates wouldn't see him and he wiped his tears on his sleeve. I smiled at him and said, "Let me show you something." I opened my drawer and pulled out a picture of myself and my husband (who is dark complexioned) and said, loud enough for his tormentor to hear, "There's nothing wrong with being dark-skinned. You just have a little more color. My husband's dark and I think it's handsome. Dark-skinned men always smell good, and they always have money." I'm not sure why I made the last comment, but I just wanted him to feel better about himself, and for some reason, I stated two qualities I liked about my husband. The other boys in the classroom looked up when they heard my remarks. The child behind my desk said, "For real? Name some dark-skinned men besides your husband who make money!" I said, "Well, there's Michael Jordan. And Michael Vick. And Morris Chestnut. And Wesley Snipes." At that moment, all of the boys that had sat with their heads down began shouting out names of successful brown or darker-complexioned men and saying things like, "He's about my color! I'm the same color as Michael Vick!" I noticed that their attitudes began to change and their chests puffed out with pride as they identified with someone successful who shared their characteristics. They did not realize that they were choosing role models to look up to and that made them feel better about themselves.

Pretty soon, word got around the school and somehow, the story took on a life of its own. I became known as the teacher that "liked dark-skinned boys." I'd be on duty at the bus stop and little chocolate boys would come over to me and say, "Are you Miz Luster? Corey said you like dark-skinned boys because they are gonna be rich. Is that true?" Word spread to even some of the upper-class students I had previously taught. Some of them would tell my students, "That's right! I was one of her favorite students! She never treated any of us different!" One day, one of my more fair-complexioned boys met me at the door, looking dejected, and asked, "Do you only like dark boys?" I hugged him and said, "No, Sweetie," and then I showed him a picture of my much lighter complexioned son. "I like ALL little boys!" That year, on Valentine's Day, I received so many gifts of cards and candy that I had to ask my husband to meet me at work to help me carry the bags home!

As the months progressed, I watched the boys try harder, and some were very successful in their studies because their positive attitude caused them to put forth more effort. My gifted student became a leader in the class, and even though he wasn't in the gifted setting, he began to shine and show his true greatness. Our test scores were much better than expected, and we exceeded our performance goals. As I recollect, I honestly think the students' attitudes were a major contributing factor. At the end of the year, we had a special program and I remember that all of my boys dressed up and wore cologne because "dark-skinned men smelled good." (In fact, they wore so much that I had to open a window to air the room out!) About a year ago, I ran into that young man that I had called behind my desk and shown the picture of my husband. He had grown up, and was doing extremely well in life. I congratulated him and let him know how proud I was. As we closed our conversation, he hugged me and then looked me directly in the eye and asked, "You remember that day you told me that dark-skinned men make money and always smell good?" I laughed and said, "Yes, and now you see I was right. You're making good money and you smell real good!" Now, I can't say that that one statement changed his life, but think about the fact that so many years later, that was the ONE THING he remembered about me. Obviously, that statement stayed with him, and changed how he viewed himself. It's quite possible that this had a ripple effect and made him now stand a little prouder, and increased his confidence and self-esteem.

This experience and many more convinced me that my calling is to inspire and motivate others. However, it took me some time to answer the call. I know that it may sound stupid, but because it seemed like second nature, I never took it seriously as a skill that could be utilized on a larger platform. If I had not faced my own mortality, I would have been content to remain in my classroom and "let the money make me" without considering that a job does not necessarily equate a life's calling. As an educator in Atlanta's inner city, I routinely used my classroom as a platform to equip my students with positive words and praise that many of them were not receiving at home. And I can also say that I have had many of these same students go on to achieve great success in life by becoming doctors, lawyers, teachers, etc. I can't count how many have reached out to me to let me know the impact I had on their lives, even when I didn't realize it. I was just being myself and treating them as I would have wanted my child to be treated — with respect and love. This made me realize that my gift was a unique part of me, and that I needed to share it with the world. In hindsight, I sincerely regret all of the years I had wasted by not pursuing my dream. That is why I am encouraging you to begin working on your dream TODAY!

Dr. West encourages all of us to "Live your BEST life!" I'd been living, but I hadn't dedicated myself to putting in the work to make my life my best life. No individual lives life to the fullest without putting forth the effort. I'm sure that many of you might be thinking, "Well, if I won the lottery, I'd definitely live my best life and the only effort that would take is buying a lottery ticket!" Well, my friend, you are wrong. Dead wrong. (Pun intended!) I recently watched Iyanla Vanzant counsel with a young woman who had won $188 million dollars and was STILL miserable. In fact, she was so downtrodden that she became depressed, abused substances, and was unable to care for her children. Money does not result in a fulfilled life. A fulfilled life must happen from within.

Once I began to answer the call, I recognized that I often procrastinated out of fear. I sometimes masked it as "I've got to do this for so-and-so," or "I'll do that tomorrow," but deep down, I felt fear. Would I be good enough? The camera adds ten pounds; was I too big to be photographed? I definitely hadn't always done the right thing; who would listen to me? Facing death is one of life's strongest reality checks, because it makes you remove the blinders and see your real life. Once I fully examined my life's path, I was able to see the potholes and bumps I had ignored along the way because I'd convinced myself that everything was smooth. I decided that if I was blessed with more life, I would use it wisely by following my dream and answering the call.

Don't make pursuing your dream a task on your "Bucket List." When Ruben asked me about following my life's calling, I was prompted to finish my book because I was considering the fact that I might die. Thanks be to God, I did not. However, if I had, that one book would have been a small contribution to make to this world, especially since I had deferred my dream for 44 years. In Langston Hughes' poem "Harlem," he poses the question: "What happens to a dream deferred? Does it dry up like a raisin in the sun?" By not pursuing my dream, I had allowed it to become stagnant and dry up inside of me. The shadow of death proved to be an impetus for me to take action, but really, that's almost like struggling to survive in the desert while a vulture stares at you. What kind of existence is that? Is that how you want to live?

I remember when I had finally finished the book. I had completed chemotherapy and was COMPLETELY bald. I was preparing to undergo seven weeks of radiation, and my goal was to get the book published in case I did not survive the entire treatment process. As I assembled the book for publication, I realized that I needed a picture for the back cover. I was too embarrassed to take one in my current state, and I pondered the decision of whether to take a headshot wearing a wig. Sure, wigs are often used by entertainers, and I had even worn them in the past for convenience. However, wigs look natural when there is a cushion of hair beneath them. When there is no base for support, wigs tend to sit awkwardly and they look obviously over-sized and unreal. I tried one on, and my husband, in his brutal honesty, told me that I looked like an extra from the original *Planet of the Apes*. I couldn't be angry and I had to laugh, because I did indeed look like a stand-in for Dr. Zira! I searched and searched for the last photo I had taken, and I finally found the picture I had sent to Dr. West, wearing a "Live Your Best Life" shirt before I had revealed my illness. Having only had 1-2 chemo treatments, my hair had not completely fallen out, and I looked more like my usual self. I cropped the photo to the neckline and used it. Each time I look at the back cover of my book, I feel that it was a divine sign of the significance of this process. Dr. West had asked me to take the photo, and he had also prompted me to finish my novel. If he had never asked me to consider my life's calling, *Coconut Cake* might have simply remained a story in my head. As you read this, ask yourself: **What will it take for you to answer the call?** Please don't wait until it might be too late, like I did, and some of your options are limited. Imagine this: If Oprah Winfrey had called me the week after my book had went to press and asked me to do a promotional tour with her, I would have had to decline because I had a weekly radiation appointment and I would have been too exhausted to travel. Now, I have to be honest with you, I would have tried my hardest to make the commitment, but that choice would have required me to compromise my mortality. I would have genuinely lost out on a once-in-a-lifetime opportunity because I had held off on my dream for so long that it had become an item on my "Bucket List." That's a high price to pay due to procrastination and fear. (Oprah, if you are reading this, I AM NOW perfectly healthy and available for any promotional tours, shows, or other opportunities you would like to discuss!)

If I could summarize my message into one word, I would use the word, "Today!" As you read, pretend that I am screaming at you, (and those of you who know me personally know that I have a very big mouth!) "TODAY! TODAY! TODAY!" Worried about what your friends might say about your dream and you're considering delaying it? Do it TODAY! Scared that your kids might get angry because they have to eat pizza while you work on your dream? Do it

TODAY! Thinking about changing your life and adopting a positive habit? Do it TODAY! Les Brown tells us that "We have to live life with a sense of urgency so that not one minute is wasted!" If there's anything that you ever wanted to do, don't put it off until tomorrow, do it TODAY! Don't allow yourself to fall into the trap that I did and **arrive at a critical destination due to procrastination**; do it TODAY! It's never too late to change; you can change TODAY!

I would like to close with a short poem that you can use for inspiration:

Tomorrow may never come; do it **TODAY!**

Opportunity that is wasted can never be replaced.

Dreams matched with effort will make them come true.

Actions that become habits will reinforce your goals like glue.

You are in charge of your destiny. Make it happen for YOU!

If this message helped you, or if you would like to connect with me, please reach out to me at:
drluster777@gmail.com, or on Facebook at Dr.Luster777, or follow me on Twitter @drluster777

Dr. Adria E. Luster

Dr. Adria E. Luster is an Atlanta-area educator that has dedicated her life to instructing at-risk children. She is a native of Kansas, and a mother of four adult children. Prior to earning her Ph.D. in Education, she earned an Educational Specialist degree, a Master's in Business Management, and a Bachelor of Arts in English.

She currently serves as an Instructional Coach by assisting teachers with delivering quality, standards-based instruction that include strategies to address the needs of both gifted and struggling learners.

Dr. Luster has presented her professional findings in various forums, both locally and nationally. She was a featured presenter at the International Organization of Social Sciences and Behavioral Research Spring Conference in 2012, as well as the 2014 Georgia Women's Conference, where she discussed her research in Women's Studies. In addition, she has volunteered within her community by providing workshops for at-risk students to prepare them for the Georgia Milestones Exam.

While battling breast cancer, Adria was encouraged to pursue her lifelong dream of becoming an author. In 2014, she published her first fictional novel titled *Coconut Cake*, using the pseudonym of Elise Massey. Her sequel, *Banana Pudding*, will be published in 2017.

Walking Through the Darkness
Rhonda Kohler

"I forgive myself for having believed for so long that I was never good enough to have, get, and be what I wanted."
—Ceanne DeRohan

"Fight or flight" is defined as the instinctive physiological response to a threatening situation, which readies one either to resist forcibly or to run away. On a cool November morning in 2011, with no fight left in me, I experienced this response and left my husband, whom I had been married to for 26 years. I had never lived on my own; I was 16 when we started dating, and 18 when we got married. At the age of 44, I was truly starting over. I realized very quickly that I really didn't even know who I was. I went from being someone's daughter to someone's wife to someone's mommy. Who was I? My identity was so engulfed in who I thought everyone wanted me to be. I nervously began the transition into "Singleness," and after being out of that particular scene for 28 years, I was completely disillusioned. I found dating to be awkward, and not something I was interested in. Being alone was hard, and as the days went on, I found myself sinking into a deep depression. I had completely shut out my family and friends. I wasn't answering phone calls or attending family get-togethers.

I remember sitting in my doctor's office about 6 months before I left. He was not just my practitioner, but a friend who I trusted and respected. Sitting in that exam room,

I shivered, not because the room was cold, but because I was finally going to share with this doctor where I was emotionally. As each minute went by, the room seemed to close in on me. My hands began to sweat even as I shivered, my ears began ringing, and panic invaded me. I was getting ready to tell someone that I did not love my husband. Something I had kept to myself far too long. I had just had my ovaries removed, and we were beginning the hormone replacement therapy. I was a wreck. I sat on that table, covered in that tiny little sheet, and sobbed. I told him how unhappy I was, and that I just wanted to be alone. He said, "Rhonda, you don't want to be alone. It's a horrible feeling." When I shared with him how I felt trapped, and that dying would be easier, he agreed that a separation would be a good idea. The most important thing was my well-being. As I left his office that day, there was a sense of relief. I had kept so many feelings bottled up for so long. Being able to finally verbalize to someone my feelings and have them validate them was a relief. So, here I was, all alone.

It's what I wanted, and I was miserable. I began to isolate myself from friends and quit going to church — something that had been a huge part of my life since I was a child. Overwhelming guilt for "tearing my family apart" began to consume me. It seemed my world was falling apart. My youngest son was struggling, and in my mind, it was my entire fault. I had to file bankruptcy. I felt so *unworthy* of anything good. That very thought caused me to attract people into my life who would only intensify that feeling and lead me into a very dark place, emotionally and spiritually. One thing my ex-husband said when I left was, "No one will ever love you. You're going to be alone with nothing." Those words echoed in my spirit many nights, and as I sat in my apartment, alone, I began to think he was right and that I deserved it.

I had lost a lot of the friends I had when I was married. I felt abandoned by people who had been a part of my life leading up to my divorce and immediately after. I was lost and broken. I would lie in bed at night, crying out to God to help me get through this. I prayed that I'd wake up and it would all just be a dream. The darkness at times was all consuming. I began to worry about everything. I was becoming so bitter and hard-hearted. These feelings were so foreign to me. I had always been someone who truly loved people, with a passion for serving and ministry. I had grown up in the church with my dad as a pastor, and by the age of 3, he had me in front of the church singing. Worship was at the core of who I was. But how was it possible for me to be effective in ministry when I was so far from God? I was in this place in my life because of choices I had made and the enemy was always right there, whispering in my ear, reminding me of all my faults.

During those days, there were weddings and new life, and I found joy in those moments, clinging to every bit of happiness I could find. I was longing for the joy that I had once known. I was so homesick, but for what? I longed for a place that I wasn't even sure existed anymore.

Has there ever been a time in your life when you felt so disconnected with the world? Have you ever been so depressed that just making it out of bed took every ounce of your strength and courage? There were days that just getting out of bed took every bit of strength I had. There was something pushing me each day, and it was truly just putting one foot in front of the other. I was simply going through the motions. Oh, I put on a brave front, and only a few who were close to me knew the emotional hell I was going through. I had stopped attending church regularly, but I knew that this was where I needed to be. The occasional times I did attend, I felt peace. It was a safe place for me, but I never allowed myself to get too connected. As soon as church was over, I would make a beeline for the door. I could never fully let go because of the sin in my life because, once again, I felt *unworthy.*

I hadn't really given that feeling a whole lot of thought until recently. I had honestly attributed it to my divorce and the mess I felt I had made. I mean, I had let so many people down: my kids, my extended family, friends, and church members. My husband was a worship leader. People looked up to us. As I began to think about these layers of feelings, emotions surfaced and I began to reach back and it took me to a 9-year-old girl — a little girl who, for her age, was heavier than the other girls. I was teased and called names by people I loved very much and by people at school. I remember how those words made me feel. I withdrew from people, never wanted to be the center of attention, and really only spoke when spoken to. In the years that followed, I put my guard up around my family members who would tease me. I was immediately defensive and I had a bad attitude, which they were quick to point out. I never felt good enough and always felt judged. I was just a little girl who wanted to be loved and accepted.

As I have become aware of the source of that feeling of being *unworthy,* it has allowed me to reflect on the choices I was making in my newly single status. I realize now that because of my desire as a little girl to be loved and accepted, but never feeling like I measured up, were the very thoughts driving me to be drawn to anyone who showed me attention. Each relationship (if you can even call them that) was leaving me empty and broken. I was searching for something that I was never going to find in any man. In each relationship, I gave a piece of myself away not just physically, but emotionally, that I could never get back. I experienced a broken heart, which no girl ever wants to have to go through. During that time of broken heartedness, I learned so much about myself, who I was, and what I wanted. I was becoming stronger. Lisa Bevere said, "The power of choice is our power to redeem our past and step into our destiny," and God was setting the stage to do an unbelievable transformation in my heart.

Steve Maraboli writes in his book, *Life, the Truth, and Being Free*, "Let today be the day you stop being haunted by the ghost of yesterday. Holding a grudge and harboring anger/resentment is poison to the soul. Get even with people, but not those who have hurt us, forget them, instead get even with those who have helped us."

I left a great deal of details out about my feelings when I left my husband, and the feeling of depression and how it manifested in my life. I did so with intention. You see, I have chosen to not live in the past because I'm so focused on my future. My past does not define me. Did I make mistakes? Yes, you better believe I did, but I am not my mistakes. I am a daughter of the most high King, and I was beginning to see myself through eyes of perfection, just as Jesus sees me. Chosen, loved, and redeemed. 1 Peter 2:9 says, "But you are a chosen race, a royal priesthood, a holy nation, a people for God's own possession, so that you may proclaim excellencies of him who has called you out of darkness into his marvelous light."

God was calling me into the light to answer my call, a call to service, specifically in worship. A call I had always known, but lost sight of… but only for a season.

Redeeming Grace
Rhonda Kohler

"When you find yourself cocooned in isolation and despair and cannot find your way out of the darkness, remember that this is similar to the place where caterpillars go to grow their wings." — Author Unknown

In August of 2014, I applied for and accepted a job in Ohio. Two of my three children had moved there, and I was excited that I would be closer to them and my grandchildren. I felt like I needed a fresh start. Looking back now, I realize that I was just continuing the pattern of fleeing from all my hurts. Like moving your hand off a hot stove, pain has a way of making us withdraw. As for me, my game of hide-and-seek from God continued.

The new job was so unfulfilling. I wasn't connecting to these people or this place. My depression was pretty severe. I was just going through the motions. I liked some of the people I worked with, but I kept them all at arm's length. I had hurt people I loved and been deeply hurt by people I loved. I had created a wall around me, and I wasn't about to let anyone penetrate the barrier I had built.

A few short months after I moved there, my daughter and son-in-law announced that they were expecting their first child, a boy! We were very excited, and I was ecstatic. As I look back on the 11 months that I lived there and pondered my purpose in moving, I'm convinced that it was to be there as my daughter navigated her way through a very difficult pregnancy that ended in an emergency C-section. I'm happy to say that she gave birth to a healthy, beautiful baby boy.

In those 11 months, my son and his family had decided to move back to Illinois. After my daughter had her baby, I said, "If there is any chance that you guys are going to move back, too, let me know because I can get my old job back." They said that they didn't feel like this would be their forever home, and they did miss family. So, with that, the decision was made that we were all coming back.

I settled right back in where I'd been prior to moving. I decided to go back to the church I had attended before I left. From the moment I walked in that first Sunday back, I knew I was home. God was calling me back to Him through His word, but especially through the worship. God was speaking to me, and the message He was clearly sending me was about His redeeming grace.

I had been carrying so much shame, and the enemy was using it to keep me from moving forward into the place God was calling me. I had missed my church. I loved the freedom there was in worshipping, and I was beginning to allow myself to be exposed, to open up, and really express all that I was during those services. As I let my guard down, the Holy Spirit revealed himself so sweetly. What I now know is that he'd never gone anywhere. He had been walking with me, and in fact, I had shut him out. Over the next few months, as I encountered God on a deeper level than ever, I was able to forgive myself, which was the key to me moving forward.

I started praying very specific prayers. "God, if you haven't forgotten about me, let this song be played today." The Lord was using my passion for worship to draw me back to Him. Bethel Music does a song, "Great are You Lord," that has become my life song. Something about it stirs my spirit, and takes me to a place of authentic communion. Anytime the enemy would try to get in my head and I started to doubt or question what God was doing in my life, that song would come on. It became His promise to me and my anthem to Him.

>You give life, You are love
>You bring light to the darkness
>You give hope, You restore
>Every heart that is broken
>Great are You, Lord
>
>It's Your breath in our lungs
>So we pour out our praise
>We pour out our praise
>It's Your breath in our lungs
>So we pour out our praise to You only
>
>You give life, You are love
>You bring light to the darkness
>You give hope, You restore
>Every heart that is broken
>Great are You, Lord

> All the earth will shout Your praise
> Our hearts will cry, these bones will sing
> Great are You, Lord (Bridge)
> — Bethel Music, "Great are You Lord"

He had brought me out of the darkness and restored my broken heart. It was truly His breath in my lungs that had gotten me through that season of despair. I would sing that bridge over and over again any time I was feeling down, defeated, or attacked, and it was changing me. These dead bones were coming alive! As I poured out my praise in every situation, God was restoring me.

I had slowly started eliminating people in my life who were not contributing to my spiritual growth. Though I had not dated anyone since moving back, there were a few who I was still allowing to occupy space in my spirit. I think maybe I was holding on to the "what if" mindset.

When I moved back, it was decided that I would start working in a service that I had very little experience in, neurosurgery, with a surgeon (who also happened to be an ordained minister) I had never worked with, Dr. Kevin Teal. The first few days back, I just observed in his room. I noticed that the music he played while working was all Christian music. I liked the atmosphere in the room; I was really looking forward to this new assignment. As I settled in as the new assistant in neurosurgery, I found that not only was I learning and growing professionally, but I was being spiritually challenged. Dr. Teal boldly spoke truth and was a man of integrity. The way he carried himself spoke clearly about his relationship with God. I looked forward to the days I worked with him. We would talk about church, music, and doing life how God had intended. I really began to trust him enough to open up and share some hurts. He would listen and give Biblical advice. It was so amazing to be able to be transparent about where I was in my faith and to have someone who just really didn't sugar coat the Word and told it like it was. He was hard on me at times, but not in a bad way. There was so much I didn't know about assisting in neurosurgery. He was challenging me to utilize my critical thinking needed to become proficient in this new service for my profession — observation, problem solving, and decision making. As I thought about that, I realized that he was also encouraging me to use critical thinking, if you will, in my "profession" as a believer — reflection, and evaluation. Was what I had been professing that I believed actually being reflected in how I was living? These revelations, both professionally and personally, were making me better and stronger in every area of my life. I was finally starting to believe that God still loved me and wanted me to be better.

    This chance assignment with this doctor I'd never met had sparked a fire in my spirit, and I was hungry for what God wanted. He was challenging me to let go of anger and bitterness, to pray for my enemies, and to walk in the light of the Lord. He reminded me weekly to "stay in my lane" — to keep my eyes fixed on the things and ways of the Lord. He checked me more than once on my attitude, reminding me that if I wanted to be part of the Kingdom that there wasn't room for hate in my heart. As the days turned to weeks, I was slowly being pointed back to the Cross. I started reading my Bible more, as well as reading books about redemption and grace. As I filled my mind with the things of the Father, the influence and voice that the last of the "what if's" had was muted. I could so clearly hear the spirit of God speaking as I allowed Him to occupy the space in my spirit.

I had started seeing quotes by Mandy Hale, a Christian author. I was really drawn to her writings and set out to find her newest book, *Beautiful Uncertainty*, about singleness, surrender, and stepping out in faith. She wrote about walking through the season of uncertainty and of idling in "The Meantime." She challenged single woman to really question whether the people who come into your life are there for a reason, a season, or a lifetime. I realized that in my loneliness, I had so desperately wanted to make people who were only passing through to teach me a lesson to be lifetime people. That had completely blinded me from my calling. I knew that there was more for me, and that God was calling me to service in worship. What I was also learning was that worship was so much more than music. I was experiencing so much growth in that truth, and I was no longer hiding from God. The Holy Spirit was revealing himself to me more every day.

"When everything else in life seems uncertain, God's presence is always a precious certainty, revealing gifts in the not knowing, the joy in the in between, and the meaning in the meantime." — Mandy Hale

I was at a movie with a girlfriend. There was a scene in the movie where the two main characters are on a first date. As they wind up the night, they are walking down the street and the guy reached over and takes the girl's hand. They exchange a sweet look and continue their stroll down the street. I looked at my friend and said, "That makes me so sad." She said, "What makes you sad?" "That," and I pointed at them walking down the street, holding hands. "I miss that," I said. In that moment, the Holy Spirit spoke to me more clearly than I had ever heard in all my years as a Christian. He said, "Sweet girl, I have been here all along. I never left you. I have been waiting for you to take my hand and walk with me." Right there in that theatre I said, "Jesus, I surrender to you. I'm ready to walk with You again."

I knew in that moment, I was forgiven and God was redeeming me. I shared that encounter with my best friend, who is the wife of a pastor. I told her that I had made the decision to not date at all anymore. I felt like God was calling me to lay aside all relationships to more clearly hear Him and follow the direction He was taking me. But I did confess to her that though I was completely surrendered, some days, it was lonely. I told her that I hoped that God would send someone who was pursuing Jesus like I was — someone I could do ministry with — and I didn't want to be alone the rest of my life. She said, "Rhonda, I believe God has someone for you, but if He didn't, would HE be enough?" I pondered that for a moment, and with a resounding "Yes," I told her, "YES, God is enough."

"What if God sees us standing there, hopeless and helpless and ensnared in the chaos of our own bad choices? And instead of turning His back on us, it makes Him long to open His arms even wider to us." — Mandy Hale, *Beautiful Uncertainty*

I was reborn. No longer a slave to fear, and free from the judgment from my own self. I was able to forgive myself, which was really the key to moving forward in serving God. I went to a prophetic worship conference and experienced the gift of prophecy. With each new gift, He was revealing to me, I realized, that God really could use me. I could be effective in ministry. With every new encounter, I ran after the Lord. I had started singing again, and led in worship with friends from a band I was in previously. I wanted so badly to be part of a worship team again. I knew in my core that this is what I'm called to do. I began to pray about it, and asked God to show me if this was the path He had for me. Not long after I began my petition to God for this affirmation, I got an e-mail from the worship leader at my church. They were going to be having auditions for their worship team! I knew that God had heard my prayer and opened up the opportunity for me to try out. I'm so excited to now be part of the Vineyard worship team. I know I am right where I'm supposed to be. I know what God's plans are for me, and I want to share the good news of what He's brought me through to everyone I can.

"I know the plans I have for you, declares the Lord, plans to prosper you and not to hard you, plans to give you hope and a future." — Jeremiah 29:11

I've come to realize that sometimes, God uses us in a way that we never expected, especially after we've walked through the darkness. There are countless examples in the Bible of where God did more with an individual after they had stepped outside of His will for them than He ever did before they started hiding from Him. I guess the point is there is nothing too difficult for my almighty God!

I stopped running and decided to answer the call on my life, a call to service through worship ministry, and it's made all the difference in the world! It has changed me and set me on a new path that has given me so much hope and a purpose.

Here are my six specific steps that I used to step into my calling after hurt, guilt, and shame plagued me and temporarily robbed me of my joy.

1. **Find someone you trust and can confide in.** You don't have to go through this alone. There is no need to try and deal with your situation alone. As individuals, we tend to see things from our own perspective. Speaking with a trusted friend, confidant, therapist, spiritual advisor, or even a relative can help us gain a new perspective on our old way of thinking.

2. **Listen to worship or inspirational music.** Music has mood altering power. The next time you're in a group, watch what happens if music is turned on — it tends to make people come alive. They start to sing, sway, and sometimes even dance. Find a special song that can

change your perspective and elevate your mood. Use it as therapy to help you get through difficult days.

3. **Find books you can read to encourage you.** There are millions of successful people who have achieved many different things and have put their strategies in books. Most of this information is available to you for under $20. It is well worth the investment, and it can give you specific strategies to change your life. You can find most of this information in audio format if you don't have the time to read.

4. **Find a church and start attending regularly.** The right church can become like an extended family where you gain a sense of belonging. This deeper connection creates additional avenues for you to learn, love, and grow. Make sure that the church you select is a loving church — not a judging church. You will feel it when it is right.

5. **Get involved in a small group or class at church.** It's not enough to just be in the church; you have to get the church in you. Worship is not a spectator sport — it is an experience that we share with our Creator. Your church home should have opportunities for you to learn and grow and gain a deeper understanding for who you are and Whose you are.

6. **Delete people in your life who are not contributing to your personal and spiritual growth therapy.** Even nature recognizes the need for separation after transformation. You never see caterpillars hanging with

butterflies. There are some people that you're just going to have to let go of. This makes room for new relationships, new experiences, and a whole new you.

I believe we all have a calling. For the sake of those who need you and are depending on you, make sure you answer the call!

Rhonda Kohler

Rhonda is a Surgical First Assistant in Champaign, Illinois. Her work ethic and ability to connect with people was instrumental in the implementation of surgical assisting in Peoria, Illinois.

The daughter of a pastor, Rhonda grew up serving others in ministry, specifically in the area of worship. Rhonda has been part of several worship teams and bands and is involved in the music ministry at her church.

Rhonda's greatest passion, however, is her family. She is the mother of 3 grown children: Ryan, Kaylyn, and Kyle, and "Mamaw" to 6 amazing grandchildren: Bennett, Noah, Cadence, Leyla, Jansen, and Rowyn.

Rhonda has a heart for ministry and worship and wants to share her passion for Christ and his message of Grace and Redemption.

You can contact Rhonda through e-mail at rkohler67@gmail.com

You can also find her on Facebook under Rhonda Ables Kohler.

Created on Purpose for a Purpose
Rosha Chandler

"You are stronger, smarter, and more resilient than you think. You are capable of achieving far more than you believe. You were meant for greatness, like all of those who have achieved it. But it takes persistence. It takes determination. It takes facing your fears and doing that which is hard and necessary." – Zero Dean

There are moments when you just know your life is about to change. The summer of 1995, as I sat on a cold table waiting for the doctor to confirm what I already knew, was one of those times. I was too naïve to fully comprehend the magnitude of the situation, but it didn't matter. It was too late for sorry's, wishing, or shoulda-woulda-coulda's. This moment was real, and there was no going backwards, only forwards. The doctor returned minutes later and confirmed the news, "You're pregnant." I imagine these announcements are usually followed by a "Congratulations," but I suppose this didn't seem like cause to celebrate.

In my world, teen pregnancy was very common, but I hadn't planned on being common. Up until that point, I'd always excelled academically, athletically, and socially. By all standards, I was on the proverbial path to success. It was either arrogance or ignorance, or maybe both, that allowed me to believe that nothing would change. I went from cheerleading to watching from the stands, from hanging out afterschool to doctors' appointments and child birth classes, and while my friends were picking out homecoming dresses, I was picking out baby strollers and cribs.

The morning of February 3, 1996, I was awakened by sharp stomach cramps. It's funny the things that stand out in your mind — what I remember most about that day is the weather; it was an unusually cold morning in St. Louis, -11 degrees to be exact. Before waking anyone, I went into the bathroom, ignoring the pangs piercing my belly. I plugged in the curlers and neatly twisted every strand of my hair. I looked in the mirror one final time as I always did before exiting the bathroom; it was the last time I ever saw that person...

On February 5, after being in labor for nearly two days, I traded in my childhood for a beautiful seven-pound, six-ounce baby boy with brown eyes and black hair.

Fast-forward Nearly Two Decades...
The knock on the door grew louder and more insistent by the minute. I was too terrified to look out the window, and I hoped it would it soon stop. What madman could be beating down my door at 5 in the morning? The knocking finally ceased, but it was replaced by the sound of chains. My frightened 9-year-old appeared from his bedroom and informed me that someone was messing with my car. I suddenly realized what was happening and my fear turned into horror. The stranger on the other side of the door was no maniac — he was the repo guy, and he had come to claim my car. The same car that I used to get to work; the same car that I used to drive my children to school and soccer practice. I jumped up, quickly threw on a robe, and half clothed I tore

out the door, but he was already heading down the street. I chased after him and he saw me in his mirror and stopped. He said there was nothing he could do and if I gave him my keys it would be easier for me in the long run, so I complied.

I WAS EXHAUSTED; physically and mentally. There are over one million words in the English language, but these three simple words were all that I could come up with to sum up the overwhelming feelings of frustration, disappointment, desperation, and sheer sadness I felt over the direction my life had taken, and more so my apparent inability to turn it around. The cliché, "life is like war," seemed like the soundtrack to my life. In its aftermath, I stood holding the pieces of a broken marriage, an unfulfilled career, and a mountain of financial obligations that I struggled to pay. Now let's be clear, I didn't walk around with my head down, depressed, and downtrodden — quite the opposite. Keeping a positive attitude was the last card I was holding, and I refused to fold, but inside I was fighting feelings of defeat, shame, brokenness, and hopelessness.

My life seemed to require more than I had to give. I felt like I was on a hamster wheel, running… running… running… yet never getting anywhere. There was no reprieve. In this world of single motherhood, breaks were a luxury I didn't have.

If my life were a movie, soft, melancholy music would be playing in the background. But this was no movie; this was life, and my kids had a front row seat to its tragic unfolding. Right on cue, the tears began to stream down my face. I wasn't crying because my car was gone. I was crying because I felt like I'd finally been beaten and worse, my son had witnessed the entire scene. I couldn't help but feel like I had failed my kids. I'd invested almost every dime and every ounce of energy I had into raising my sons. But for every dollar I invested or word of wisdom I'd offered, what had my life taught them? What had they learned by simply watching how I lived?

Chipping Away

Life as a single teen mom was anything but easy. Learning what it meant to be grown up while helping someone else grow up (and by helping, I mean being completely responsible for) is a quite a feat. I guess hard wasn't good enough; I liked things to be really hard because less than two years after my first son was born, I gave birth to another baby boy. Perhaps Langston Hughes described it best in his poem, "Mother to Son," best known for its famous line: "Life for me ain't been no crystal stair." My life certainly wasn't. It was messy and far more complicated than it needed to be, but I was fighter and I refused to give up. Despite what statistics said about single teenage moms and their children, my children inspired me. I wouldn't accept what the world wanted to give us. They said I was more likely to end up living in poverty and worse, the little boys whose tiny fingers I traced at night as they slept while watching their tiny chests rise and fall as they took gentle breaths were more likely to drop out of school and end up in prison. God impressed upon my heart that He could have chosen anyone in the world to be their mother, and He choose me so I knew they couldn't be the reason (or excuse) I didn't succeed; they were the reason I had to. Through it all, I managed to be a good mom, go to school full time, and within 5 years, I completed my Bachelor's with honors and was offered a salary position in the advertising department of a well-known department store.

In theory, things were looking up, but in reality, I'd survived the last 5 years on a part-time salary that was heavily subsidized by credit cards, student loans, and government assistance, which I no longer qualified for. To top it off, I needed to purchase a reliable car (and no, I didn't buy a new car) and I made the decision to put my boys in private school. A large number of the schools in the St. Louis area were battling issues with low test scores, accreditation, and even violence, so I was going to send my boys to private school, no matter the cost.

"The ground is no place for a champion."
— Muhammad Ali

The next 20 years would bring a tumultuous marriage that ended in divorce after 10 years, serious financial difficulties, and the harsh reality that I'd invested almost 15 years in a career that wasn't a good fit. At every turn, it appeared I failed. I'd fallen down A LOT, (primarily due to poor choices) and there were many times I wanted to stay down, but every time I stood at that crossroad something inside of me wouldn't let me quit. I'm guessing you're the same way, and that's why you're reading this.

No matter how many times we fall, we HAVE to get back up. But getting up is just the start. Moving past a setback or overcoming a problem is simply winning the battle, but there's an entire war to be fought if we are going to truly be victorious. Some challenges we come up against leave behind a residue (also referred to as scars) that lingers long after the problem is gone — taking up residence in our minds, slowly chipping away at our identity, our dreams, our confidence and our hope for a better future. Business failed... chip... bankruptcy... chip.... foreclosure... chip... abuse... chip... divorce... chip... Everything we deem a "failure" slowly chipping away at us until eventually, we wake up and the reflection we see in the mirror is that of a stranger. The two big brown eyes that stared back at me didn't belong to a girl who fought her way through college while raising two small kids on her own. Instead, they belonged to a woman whose car had been repossessed; a woman who hated her job, was divorced, and barely getting by. This is how I now saw myself. I believe what keeps us from living our dream isn't what happens to us; it's how we see ourselves as a result. We're left wondering, "What happened to me?" Where is the girl with bold confidence who dared to believe she could do anything, or the boy with audacious dreams who was going to take the world by storm?

Once you were going to change the world; now you can't manage to lose 5 lbs. You're holding on to the very end of hope, but your reality feels too big to ignore. You repeated a hundred, if not a thousand times, "You're a lender and not a borrower," yet you owe more money than you think you could ever pay. You told yourself nothing is impossible for you and everything you touch is blessed, but your business, your finances, and your relationships have fallen apart. You might not ever say it out loud, but inside you think, maybe, just maybe you can't lose the weight, you can't have a successful business, you'll never have the spouse of your dreams. Maybe successful people are lucky, or maybe they were born with something inside of them that allows them to be successful that others don't. Maybe there is an "it" and whatever "it" is, you don't have.

Created on Purpose for a Purpose

By late 2014, I was reaching my breaking point. Every day, I had to mentally talk myself off the ledge and I didn't think I could hold on much longer. When I was in college, God gave me a vision that I would have a platform to talk to and empower women. Over a decade later, when this still haven't come to fruition, the small glimmer of hope I held felt more like a burden to carry than a promise of a better tomorrow. I was convinced the only thing worse than losing hope was holding on to false hope.

Around this time, while attending my usual Sunday service, I heard the words, "I AM HER" in my spirit and I was lead to Psalms 139:13-14 — "You formed my inmost being, you knit me together in my mother's womb. I praise you because I am fearfully and wonderfully made." There was so much wisdom in those three simple words that I can't share it all in this book, but there were two key lessons that I will share with you. I really hope you take this to heart because these aren't just words on a page. If you truly understand this, it should be life changing. The first lesson, "You formed my inmost being, you knit me together in my mother's womb," meaning you were created on purpose for a purpose. This began before you were even born, so your purpose is so much bigger than you are and NOTHING you could EVER do could change that (your actions can keep you from it but it can't change it). We can look at it from a practical stand point. Most, if not all of us, are familiar with Prince William, the son of Prince Charles and Princess Diana. He isn't royalty because of anything he's done; he is a prince because it's his birthright and this destiny was in place long before he was ever born.

The second lesson, "I am fearfully and wonderfully made," means that despite your shortcomings, despite the mistakes you've made (no matter how many), despite how your situation looks or how you feel, you are equipped and able to do what you were called to do. We can use another practical example. When a car is created, the manufacturer builds it with its intended purpose in mind. They put everything inside the car that it needs to function as it is intended and God has equipped us the same way. YOU were meant to pay for that single mom's groceries; YOU were meant to buy your mom the house she never could afford; YOU were meant to build orphanages and playgrounds around the world.

Now, let's keep it real, even with this revelation, I woke up with the same amount of money in the bank, the same job and the same challenges, but now I had this "thing" ignited inside me that I couldn't ignore (and believe me, I tried sometimes). It was no longer a question of could I do it — it was a matter of I must do it. I was created to fulfill this mission, to empower women (especially single moms) to live a life of purpose; who was I to walk away, who was I to change the script? It's like being drafted to war. You are not asked; you are called to this mission greater than yourself to make life better for others. Your purpose is not even about you.

Closing the Gap
Rosha Chandler

"The space between where I am and where I want to be inspires me." — Tracie Ellis Ross

What do we do now? The distance between where we are and where we need to go can seem so big. It can be enough to stop us before we get started. Can we really do it? How do we possibly get from here to there? The answer is simple — you start. I'd like to share six tips that I used to get me moving in the right direction. Before I do, I want to make sure you are going into this with the right motivation. If your motivation for what you're currently pursuing is only (or mostly) money, stop now! If you're chasing money, that is exactly what you will be doing 20 years from now. Stop chasing money and chase your dreams. Money isn't the goal; money is the reward for achieving your goal, which should be to walk in your purpose. Many people invest their time in becoming someone they were never meant to be, and as a result they are overwhelmed, frustrated, and flat out unhappy. It's only when you learn to leverage the gifts and talents within that you will achieve true success and happiness.

Step One

Clarity is key… The first thing you must do is get clear about what you were created to do. If you fail to do this step, none of the others will matter. Think of it this way — imagine you have somewhere important to be. You pull into the parking lot right on time, only to realize you're at the wrong location. The fact that you arrived means nothing if you're in the wrong place.

The key to your individual success is found in the question, *what makes me unique?* God placed something on the inside of all of us that He wants us to give away to the world; some people refer to it as a blueprint or a seed. Consider an apple and an orange tree — they thrive in different conditions. If you identify the seed, you know what is required to nurture and grow it. Who you are on the inside should align with what your life looks like on the outside. When you cultivate the seeds within, you can blossom into the best version of yourself. Spend time getting clear about who you are and what you want your life to look like.

Take Action Now... Write a vision statement. Writing a vision statement is the first step to focusing your life; it states the desired outcome you want and should reflect your values, goals and purpose. It serves as your roadmap and provides the direction for your life.

Create a vision statement for each area of your life (2-3 sentences). Each statement should communicate what you would like to be, do, or have. I recommend scheduling some time with yourself and doing this in a space where you feel inspired; the park, a coffee shop, or the library.

Step Two
Write your goals... Now that you have a vision for your life, it's time to set goals that will make that vision a reality!

Take Action Now... Take each vision statement and list every goal needed to accomplish your desired outcome. Be sure to make S.M.A.R.T. goals (specific, measurable, achievable, realistic, and timely).

Step Three

Pick one goal to focus on... I know you have a big vision for your life, and focusing on one goal seems like it just won't cut it! But if you try to focus on all of them at the same time, chances are you'll struggle to give your goals the time and energy needed to see the progress you're hoping for. Focusing on one big goal doesn't mean ignoring all your other ones. It just means you decide what is most important and where you will spend the bulk of your available time and energy (because you only have so much). My #1 goal is to build a profitable business, so that is where I focus most of my energy, but that doesn't mean that I ignore my goal of improving my health and neglect exercising. It's a question of what's most important to you at this moment in your life, and which one of your goals would have the biggest impact. Just ask yourself — what's the first thing that comes to mind when you think about creating a better life for yourself and your family? Is it getting out of debt, starting a business, losing weight? **Let me caution you — be very careful!** As soon as you make up your mind to pursue a goal, fear will creep in disguised as confusion and you'll ask yourself questions like, *what if I didn't pick the right goal? What if this isn't the right path for me?* Stop it! The land of "what if's" is the place where dreams go to die.

Take Action Now... Schedule some quiet time to review all your goals and reflect on where you need to see a breakthrough first in your life. Are you experiencing serious financial problems? Do you have health concerns? Be sure to get to the root of the problem. For example, I've started having issues with my blood pressure; obviously, nothing is more important than your health, so the initial assumption could have been I needed to make health my number one priority. However, I know my stress primarily came from financial pressure and my job, so it was easy for me to see that building a profitable business was the best thing I could do for myself at this point in my life. By accomplishing that one goal, I've solved my job and financial problems and ultimately my health concerns. Elect the one goal you will pursue and put it somewhere that you will see it often. I suggest making it your screen saver on your phone and/or computer.

Step Four

Write your "Why Statement"... You must have a strong "why" behind what you're doing. This is another essential step because no matter how much you want something and how many good reasons you have to do it, there will be more opportunities to quit than to keep going. Your "why" should motivate you in difficult moments. I think we lose sight of the fact that our goals are bigger than us and when we quit, we're not just quitting on ourselves, but on our families and all the people whose lives we were meant to impact.

Take Action Now... Write your Why Statement. It can be one thing or a list. Mine are written in paragraph form. You can also add quotes or pictures that inspire you. The format isn't important. The point is to make it strong enough to drive you when nothing else will.

Step Five
Make a Plan... *"A goal without a plan is just a wish"* — Antoine de Saint-Exupery. Now that you've identified the goal to focus on and the reason you must do this, it's time to create a step-by-step action plan using a method known as "chunking." The power of chunking is creating small, achievable steps. By chunking your goals, you create a daily action plan that is moving you forward, creating momentum and building your confidence. No more being all over the place and wondering why you aren't making any progress. Be strategic, focused, and consistent.

Take Action Now... Start with the end result in mind. Write out smaller goals and then break them into smaller steps. For example, if your end result is to start a business, your first goal might be to choose the right business, and steps would include things like research, or maybe contacting certain people. Your second goal could be to write a business plan, and steps would include things like finding a template, research, etc. Keep adding small goals, broken into steps, until you've mapped a complete plan. Next, determine the time needed for each task and assign a deadline. Your task list will serve as your daily action list. Of course, as you learn, this will be adjusted. But having this plan WITH STEPS gives you things to do every day and a sense of accomplishment as you check things off your list and move closer to your goal! The important thing is doing something every day.

Step Six

Do the work consistently... "Success doesn't come from what you do occasionally, it comes from what you do consistently" — Marie Forleo. This has been a big struggle of mine, and I've questioned if I could do it. I used to wish that I would wake up one day and things would suddenly click. I wondered, what is that moment for people where they go from being stuck to realizing their dreams? What happens in that space between stuck and realization? Whatever it is, why can't it happen for me? Have you ever wondered that? The answer is consistency — **consistency happens**. Oprah Winfrey said, "The big secret in life is there is no secret. Whatever your goal, you can get there if you're willing to work."

Start Now

"Start where you are. Use what you have. Do what you can" — Author Ashe. You don't need more money, more talent, or more resources. You simply need to get started. Think of the people standing on the other side of your blessing, the people you were meant to reach (this includes your kids and your family). Do you really want to leave this earth never having done what you were put here to do in the first place?

Rosha Chandler

Rosha Chandler holds many titles, including published author, speaker, entrepreneur, but her most esteemed title is mother of three. Born and raised in St. Louis, she became a mom at the tender age of 18. While this created challenges, it is through this challenge that she discovered her God-given purpose, which is to empower, educate, and connect with women who faced similar circumstances.

Rosha embarked upon a new journey in 2016, launching Chasing Butterflies, a company dedicated to helping single and working moms create the business and life they love. As a hardworking mother herself, she knows all too well the challenges in raising a family and building a business, and she is committed to helping women successfully navigate their course.

She holds a Bachelor's Degree in Business & Marketing and a Master's Degree in Creative Writing.

Rosha hopes to one day share her message and inspire women all over the world. When she isn't working, Rosha enjoys volunteering at her church and in the community. Most importantly, she loves spending quality time with her family and friends. She is also a member of Toastmasters International.

Email: simplyrosha@gmail.com
Facebook: https://www.facebook.com/chasingbutterflies01

Move Forward... And Don't Look Back
Angie Hodges

"We must be willing to let go of the life we planned, so as to have the life that is waiting for us."
— Joseph Campbell

There have been multiple times in my life where I knew it was time for me to answer the call and make a change. Sometimes, it is a call we are looking forward to, and sometimes, it's a call that we would rather not answer. On January 28, 2011, I answered the call and filed for divorce. The court hearing was at 9 a.m. It was cold, and what I really wanted to do was curl back up, stay in bed, and sleep. I felt so tired and a weariness that I had never felt before; my energy was low and my stomach was in knots from anxiety. There was an ache in my heart that I so desperately needed to go away. My appetite was gone and this nightmare didn't seem to be ending anytime soon. About 8:30 a.m., I realized that I should get going; I didn't want to be late. Too many thoughts and emotions were overwhelming me. This was supposed to last forever. I asked myself, "How did we get here... we didn't start out this way. What happened to the love, the good times... what happened to us?"

I don't know... I had been trying to figure that out for many years, trying to make sense of it. We had issues off and on, but by 2008, it escalated to a continuing saga of drama and chaos. In the beginning, we both made a genuine effort to work on the marriage. As the years went on, he checked out, became intentionally disrespectful, hateful, and didn't care what I thought or how I felt. What was he getting out of it, I don't know. But what's worse is what was I getting out of it. Was I hoping that if I bled on the cross of this dysfunctional relationship that one day, he would wake up and realize he didn't want to lose me or his family, completely change, and life would be wonderful? Or was I sitting and waiting for "someone" to confirm and validate that I didn't deserve this? Was I wishing "someone" would feel that I was valuable enough, worthy enough to stand up for me? Did I think "someone" would save our marriage and help put it back together again? Was I hoping "someone" could get through to him and show him that he was dishonoring me as his wife and the mother of his children? Was I looking for "someone" to love me enough to rescue me? It's the part where the knight in shining armor saves the day, the "someone." That all sounds possible in a fairytale, this was real life. But that "someone" actually did come. And she came to rescue me! She took her power back, and finally boldly stepped up and handled her business! That "someone" was ME!

"Angie," my lawyer tapped me on my shoulder and said, "Let's go on in." Feeling faint, I walked in and sat on that hard, wooden courtroom bench in Boone County courthouse, listening to the cases, hearing stories about other families being torn apart. What I didn't realize then was just how many times that I would be there sitting and talking to God, pleading with Him for this to be over, and needing Him to ease the pain. But here I am, sitting in this courthouse holding my Bible, praying, going over scriptures, trying to take my mind anywhere but here. This wretched room is full of lawyers, the bailiff, the court reporter, and the judge; it just all feels sick. They look like actors in a bad movie. To combat the feeling, I just start picking people to pray for. I see some soon-to-be ex-couples sit by each other, some with no lawyer that just walk up and let the judge know what they want to do. They are actually friendly. Then there is the man that walked in with his new girlfriend, who sneers at the wife as if she has won some type of prize; he has a smirk on his silly face. They both look so disgusting. Every one of these married couples went to some venue and vowed to love each other for life; the room is filled with broken promises. A sterile and impersonal stench fills the air. I told myself to stop asking God why this is happening to me, but to please show me the lesson because I never want to do this again. I'm holding my breath; my body feels so tense. Somehow, my feet were walking and before I knew it, I was in front of the judge, hoping that he would feel some type of compassion, knowing that he would be making some really important decisions about the lives of me and my children. The lawyers made their comments and about 7 minutes later, I am walking out. I wonder, does he feel as miserable as I feel right now? My lawyer gives me a paper with my next court date and says we'll talk before then. I rush to my cold car and just sit there numb and wondering, "What I do now?"

    I did not know the direction that my life was going, what I would do, who I was supposed to be, how this change would affect my life, or even how I would take care of my children. I just knew I had to move forward, and there was no going back. It wasn't something that I wanted, but living life as I had been and continuing to raise my children in an unhealthy environment was no longer an option. I was scared. I did not completely understand God's plan, but I had encountered Him enough to know that I would have to trust that He was in control. My faith in Him was so much bigger than the fear in my heart.

We all will have a season or time in our lives where we are faced with the obstacle of having to change and do something different than the life we planned. My story is about taking back my life and CREATING and DEFINING it on my own terms. Falling in love with myself, getting in touch with the person I left behind, and establishing a new and even more beautiful relationship with that her. I had to figure out how to create a new life as a single woman. I discovered how to not merely survive, but to thrive. I am not victim, but a victor who overcame in the face of adversity. And as it says in Isaiah 61:3, He is turning my ashes into a crown of beauty.

We all have our challenges. Maybe you're a professional who's been in the same career for many years, now having to deal with the voluntarily or involuntarily task of defining a new career path. Or possibly you have hit the glass ceiling, experienced a layoff, or are no longer happy with where you are and have to figure out what do next. Maybe you are the couple that waited to plan your family at just the right time, and are excited that your new baby is on the way. But when you go to the doctor's office, you learn that your child has a medical issue that requires a lot of attention. What do you do? Or are you the person that had diligently saved a nest egg, only to encounter a huge financial loss, a setback, or an unexpected emergency? How will you get through that? Or perhaps the love of your life was diagnosed with a terminal illness, and you dread losing your best friend. Forever was supposed to last longer. How do you go on? None of us is exempt from adversity in life.

Sometimes, to figure out where you're going, you might have to examine where you've been. How did I even get to this point? What events in my life occurred to lead me, right here and right now, to the intersection that I am at? Well, for me, I lived in a new home subdivision in rural Illinois. This was a stark contrast to being raised by my single mom in the inner city of Milwaukee. My family was full on love, but usually lacking on financial resources. When I got married, most of the time I was stay-home mom, and had given up my career to raise our children. Family time was a priority for both of us in the beginning, but as time went on, the kids were usually with me. We lived with our 4 children in a beautiful, huge, 3,100-square-foot home — over 4,500 square feet with the basement. We had built two brand new homes from the ground up within the first 5 years of marriage. I picked the lot, floor plan, design, colors, and the amenities. My bedroom alone was the size of some entire apartments. To our family and friends, we were like George and Weezy and had moved on up. Living a life that I had imagined, but prior to living it, didn't know anyone that did. We both came from families with a lot of broken marriages and single parents. I prayed we would break the chains of generational curses and create a new paradigm for ourselves and our children instead of reliving them. We had our ups and downs throughout the years, but I always thought we would make it. We had to. Luther Vandross talked about it when he sang, "But a room is not a house and a house is not a home. When the two of us are far apart. And one of us has a broken heart," and my heart was broken.

I used to think that idolatry only meant worshiping a statue. I didn't realize that it could be anything. In my case, I worshipped my husband, my children, my marriage, and my life. I had put everything into them, and lost myself along the way. I could barely hold a conversation without talking about my husband or kids. But my marriage was still on the downward spiral and became a ship with big gaping holes that no matter how much I tried to patch, it was leaking somewhere else. As mothers and wives, we think it is admirable to give, give, and give until we have nothing, many times feeling that the more we neglect ourselves, the more of a superwoman we are. I placed him on a pedestal that he had no place being. I saw so much potential in him, in us, in the kids, and somehow forgot about me. I did not honor the amazing woman that I am! I placed too little regard on all that I brought to the table. I hid behind my husband and children. and did not fully operate with the gifts I had been blessed with, preferring to focus on them. Have you ever wanted something to work so badly that you would do almost anything, even sacrificing your own self-respect?

I had to have everything stripped away and become naked before God. That pruning process was very painful, as people and things were removed from my life. I was literally dying inside, screaming with no sound coming out, and the people around me couldn't even tell. And if they could... I didn't know. Sometimes, the strongest people don't know how to ask for help. I felt alone. Everyone looks at you and figures you have it together. When I finally got to a place that I did ask for help, they still didn't really get it. Family and friends that I thought would be there looked the other way, didn't know what to do, or preferred not to get involved. It was only by the grace of God that I did not lose my mind. He kept me. My mind, body, and spirit were broken. I felt like I was sleeping with the enemy. I always knew I deserved better; my kids deserved a better example of a marriage. I just couldn't figure out how to bridge the gap between what I was experiencing and what I knew was God's best for me. I continued to parent, mustering my strength to pour the good I had into our children while avoiding confrontations.

I was transitioning to a single mom with 4 kids, and I was irritated. Don't get me wrong, my kids are my best blessings and I love them dearly, but this isn't what I signed up for. It was supposed to be a shared responsibility. Instead, I was doing the parenting while he stepped in when it fit his schedule. The children were a major factor for me staying, and also a major factor for me leaving. How would this affect them? If it were not for them, I would have been gone a long time ago. I wanted my children to be raised in a loving, two-parent home. As their parents, we owed it to them. I did not want them to have to experience the complete upheaval of the life they knew. But, even more importantly, I had to make the choice if it would be more detrimental to have them to deal with divorce, or have them grow up witnessing a dysfunctional marriage. I did not want them to think that what they heard and saw was normal. This was no example for them to follow. No more — not on my watch. I knew better, and it was time for me to do better. When I felt like I couldn't go on, and like I wanted to give up, I'd look in their eyes and know that they were counting on me. Many times, that is all that kept me going. With all that was wrong in my life, being a good mom to them was something that I was doing right. I needed to be strong for them and for myself. There were many days that I was overwhelmed and did not know if I was coming or going. But a wise woman told me that if I could just manage to keep it together in front of them, they would be okay. I was their anchor now, and I had to remain stable.

But also tell you the truth, I was mad as hell! I gave 15 years of my life, loving him and our children, taking care of our family, and sacrificing for this? There is no justification! If a person wants to move on, it is honorable to do it as peacefully as possible. There was no need for it to end the way it did, the perpetual chaos our family life had become. I was married to a man stuck in an adolescent boy's behavior: selfish, spoiled, manipulative, ignoring responsibilities, having temper tantrums, and taking it for granted that I would clean up the mess. I was trying to have a loving, mutual relationship with someone who was emotionally unavailable to love me. Narcissistic personality types are charming and appear to be the ideal mate, which makes it even harder for people to believe what you are experiencing; it can have you doubting your own reality. I would question myself, wondering if I was making this up in my head. I didn't know who would be coming home from work — some nights would it be Dr. Jekyll, and others it was Mr. Hyde. My prayer to God was to fix him or move him.

In the meantime, it was time for me to get off of this crazy-making roller coaster. I came to the realization that enough was enough. Oprah said, "If a person shows you that they do not want you or value you, then release them." I released him into the stratosphere and kept it moving. No one can tell you at what point that is for you. I believe marriage is a life-long commitment. Also, by that same token, there are too many people suffering in the church in seriously unhealthy situations that are risking not only their health, but their safety and their children's safety. They are being held hostage by guilt, shame, fear, and condemnation. If you are in a situation that is detrimental to you spiritually, emotionally, mentally, or physically... leave. That does not mean it cannot be restored. But I do believe that God wants you to be healthy and whole. He wants His best for you. It took me many years to get the revelation that it was time to let go.

The more I have walked this journey, the more I've learned that the real obstacle was not about our divorce or him; it was about me answering the call to be the woman that God called me to be. This is about my restoration, renewal, and rebirth! Beauty can be birthed from the ugliest situations. Sometimes, I don't recognize the woman I've transformed into! God had already determined my destiny, and He allowed me to go through this thorny situation so I could use it as a catalyst for my growth. People had to be moved out of the way so that He could do the real work on me. I can see the good in all of this, because I don't know if I would have become the woman I am today without the hell I lived through. I became better, not bitter. See, there is actually no one to blame. I have forgiven him and myself; both people contribute to the breakdown of a marriage. I can truly say that I wish him God's best, because with no tests, there can be no testimony.

"Adversity causes some men to break, and others to break records." — William Arthur Ward

As to how the day ended on January 28, 2011 —that day at the courthouse was only the beginning. I walked in and out of that courthouse for 4 long years. I didn't realize at the time that even when my divorce was over, it would still continue, but that is another story.

There's a song called "Greater is Coming" by Jekalyn Carr, and my greater is coming, it is right now! I want you to know that no matter what circumstances you are facing, or challenges that come against you, your greater is coming, too. Keep pressing and seek Him. Let go of what was, walk into what awaits you, and let your light shine!

Shine Bright
Angie Hodges

"You are a light. And when you shine, you shine bright." — Marie Lu, *The Midnight Star*

Unlike the weather outside, you choose how brightly you shine every day. Are you dreary and dismal, do you have patches of light, or do you turn it up and shine bright like the high sun on a clear day? Every day is a blessing and an opportunity for you to be your highest self and Live Your Best Life! The world needs you and your contribution! Yes, you!

I have seen far too many people become bitter over life, and especially over failed relationships. Because we are relationship-oriented, disruption in our relationships can throw off our entire life if we let it. I know you know people like this. Based on what someone did or said, they resolve to never be the same. You can see it all over them — the mean mug, their negative and closed-off energy. Nothing going out, and nothing coming in. If that happened to you, I am sorry that it did. I mourn with you; grieving is definitely a process. But, you owe it to yourself to live! Appreciate and embrace every day! You may have been in a relationship with someone with a gambling problem, suffering from depression, or an alcoholic. You might have been lied to, cheated on, and completely disrespected. I empathize with the pain that you have gone through and that you feel. But you must continue to go on and live! In fact, I don't just want you to live, I want you to live out loud! Shine bright until others around you need to put on their sunglasses! Your significant other may have moved on, possibly with multiple people or even impregnated someone else and is trying to keep you along for the ride. You cannot give them any more of your valuable time worrying about what they're doing. You have to do you! If you keep looking backwards, you will miss the opportunities in front of you and continue to experience pain. The best payback you can give anyone is to leave them alone! Spend absolutely no time thinking or worrying about that other person. Move on, and let God deal with them.

It is easy to assume that everything will get easier, when you do. Wrong. Unfortunately, it may become more difficult, but hold on. Sometimes, when you chase your own happiness, people can become even more ugly, vindictive, and evil because you are ignoring them. But chase it, I mean run full steam ahead. Embrace your power.

I don't even like to tell my story because it requires too much of my time looking in the rearview mirror at situations that I would much rather forget. I am too focused on being the best me today and preparing for my journey ahead. But if anything from my story can help or inspire one person, then it was not in vain. God has blessed me in so many ways, and I can never stop thanking Him and telling others how He delivered me! I smile every day because I'm happy — not because my life is perfect, but because God blessed me with an opportunity to live another day.

There are 6 steps I used to overcome my obstacles, answer the call, and live my best life. It is possible at some point in your life you may reach a season where you need to reinvent yourself and define a new way of being because your current way of living no longer works. These are easy to follow steps that will help you overcome difficulties and be victorious in the challenges you are facing. There are many different situations that you will encounter on your journey, but my hope for you is that these steps will empower you to answer the call and Live Your Best Life!

1. Know Thyself.

Fall in love with the amazing, awesome, and wonderful you! Get to know yourself. I'd focused so much energy on my family that I really had lost touch with who I was. I mean, I could implement plans and create strategies for everyone in my house. I could see clearly what they needed to do. Praise the Lord when I finally learned how to turn the attention on myself! I had to learn who I was and what I liked to do.

Ask yourself these or similar questions:
- What things did I like to do before I became a husband, wife, mother, etc.?
- Are there other areas that I wanted to explore but I put off because of other circumstances?
- If I could do anything with no regards to money, time, or other people, what would I do?
- Who am I?
- What is my purpose?

- What am I good at?
- When am I at my happiest?
- What are some areas of my life that I would like to improve?

I have posed a lot of questions to you, and I want you to get out a piece of paper and start writing — don't censor it. Just write freely. You might be amazed at what you see.

I also spent time in the scriptures, reading about who God says I am. Repeat the following scriptures out loud, with conviction, and the knowledge that they are about you! These are just a few things that God says about you:

- I am complete in Him who is the Head of all principality and power. (Colossians 2:10)
- I am far from oppression, and fear does not come near me. (Isaiah 54:14)
- I am born of God, and the evil one does not touch me. (1 John 5:18)
- I have the mind of Christ. (1 Corinthians 2:16; Philippians 2:5)
- I have the peace of God that passes all understanding. (Philippians 4:7)
- I have the Greater One living in me; greater is He Who is in me than he who is in the world. (1 John 4:4)

Affirmations are great to use. They are sentences that speak positively about what you want for your life, but are written in the present. Affirmations are not about what you don't want, but speak of what you desire your reality to be right now. Write some affirmations for yourself — these can be for many different areas of your life. Here are some examples:

Everything works out for my highest good. I am beautiful and smart. This day brings me nothing but joy. I am a money magnet and attract wealth and abundance. My relationship is healthy and loving. I let go of worries that drain my energy. The answer is right before me, even if I am not seeing it yet. I do work that I love and I am paid well for it.

I actually printed out about 10 pages of scriptures, quotes, and affirmations that spoke to me about who I am. I taped them to my kitchen cabinets and on doors throughout my house. Pick out scriptures and create affirmations that apply to you. You can write these in a journal, create a poster, put them on post-it notes on your bathroom mirror or refrigerator, or on note cards to carry with you. The main thing is to select a place or a style that best fits your life so that you can repeat them daily.

2. Utilize the Experts.
Many times, we are ashamed and do not want to share what we are going through with others. But if you have not been successful in making the changes you need please utilize experts. Reach out to a therapist, your pastor, or join a support group. There are also national support groups for Alcoholics Anonymous, Grief Recovery, Children and Adults with Attention Deficit Disorder, Divorce Care, Single & Parenting, Financial Peace University, Codependents

Anonymous, etc. that help in different areas of your life. Needing help is nothing to be ashamed about, but there is something to be ashamed of in needing help and not seeking it. I am proud to say that I received help from pastors, support groups, and had a therapist who helped me get through the process, encouraged me, and gave me an objective perspective. I attended Single & Parenting, Financial Peace University, and Divorce Care. It is perfectly good to seek professionals to sort through difficult phases of our lives. Coaches are also excellent resources. There are general life coaches or coaches for specific needs — career development, physical fitness, etc. Schedule consultations with at least three professionals to find someone who will be a good fit. When you need your car worked on or your eyes checked, you go to people that have been trained in that occupation. Most of the time, your family is biased, and your friends are going through the similar situations and won't give you the most objective advice.

3. Create the Vision.

Believe it, see it, speak it, meditate on it, write it, and eventually, you live it. I made vision and gratitude boards. I also created a new form of journaling called Destiny Journaling, which is writing that speaks into your future. For many people, journaling can be just rehashing of problems, which can be helpful. But Destiny Journaling is based on calling new things into existence. Gratitude is so very important. You can use a gratitude board or journal, and just start writing everything that you are thankful for, no matter how big or small. Do it regularly, like each morning before you get up or at night before bed. When we are in a bad place or circumstance, it is so easy to focus on the negative or what is missing. Instead write down what you are thankful for.

For your vision boards, write words and cut out pictures that symbolize what you envision for your life. The outcome doesn't always match up exactly, because God determines how it will come to pass. When I first started doing my vision boards, I put career, education, family, vacation, and relationship goals on there, and quite a bit of other stuff. Close your eyes and imagine your life as you would like to experience it, visualize the details in your mind's eye. You need to see yourself doing what you want to do — how will it feel, how will it look and smell, how will you act, will anyone else be there with you, what are the other sensory perceptions that you will experience when engaging in this activity — and purposely think about this daily. Dream big! Don't put a cap on what you can achieve.

"Set a goal to achieve something that is so big so exhilarating that it excites you and scares you at the same time." — Bob Proctor

Writing down your dreams, goals, and plans is not enough. You have to take action steps and implement them, or it's just a lot of wishful thinking on paper. Action steps will provide you with the necessary course of action to implement your goal. Be detailed with your steps and determine a time frame for each one. Goals need to have a birthdate or a time range for completion to help you stay on task and monitor progress. Sometimes, the date will have to be revised. What are the steps it will take to get you from where you are today to where you want to be?

4. Maintain Self Care

Fill up your own tank. Take the time to be still, pray, and meditate. When you have a lot going on in your life, many times, you can't hear God because of all of the chaos. There are times that you might feel like God isn't talking to you, but maybe it's that you need to sit still so that you can hear Him.

Self-care can be different things for different people. Listening to music, working out, painting, sewing, making an appointment with a nutritionist, or crocheting are just a few examples. Do you like to get massages to ease the tension? A community college in my area offered massages by the students, and I went there regularly to just help take the edge off. Our bodies hold stress. Health is key when experiencing ongoing stress, which is detrimental to the body.

Taking care of yourself also means scheduling your annual checkups. When you have a lot going on in your life, it is easy to put medical appointments to the back of the "to do" list. Dr. Elisha Robinson-Asiso is the founder and owner of Integrative Healing Center, in Rockford, IL. She said, "There is a correlation between stress and your physical and spiritual health. Self-care is also about forgiveness. You must fully forgive. Unforgiveness keeps you from moving forward and opens you up to spiritual attacks on your body. Everything you do is spiritual, and some diseases are spiritual diseases. Cancer has a spiritual component. Speak healing over your bodies, watch your eating habits, do the work, remember that your body is your temple, and gluttony is a sin." What will you do to start the process of self-care for yourself?

5. Have Fun!

Enjoy your life! With all of the things that we have to do, we often forget to have fun. Some people don't even know what they would do for fun. It's not a bad word. Be willing to step out of the box. Yes, we have responsibilities and things to take care of, but please take a moment to smile, laugh, and do something that you enjoy. And if you don't know what fun is for you, then have fun figuring it out. Take a look at meetup.com — it is a free site with tons of activities and groups based on interests all around the country. I have gone to a quite a few and met some good people. Also, setting aside time to do absolutely nothing is extremely fun.

Another love of my mine that I decided to make time for is travel. Since I filed for divorce, I traveled to 13 cities and out of the country, either with my children, friends or solo. Now, I do realize it is possible that traveling with your family can create a financial strain. This is when you get creative. What day trips or weekend trips would you be interested in taking? Many times, there are tourist attractions in our own city that we have never seen and some have free days for residents. There are many beautiful parks, forest preserves, and trails to enjoy. Where do you want to go? What do you want to do? Figure it out and get going!

6. Seek New Opportunities

You have to be open and looking. I replied to a Facebook post seeking hosts and began hosting my own radio show, "Bfabulous," on a new startup, SOAR Radio, which has since become a Stellar Award Nominee. I came up with the name because I wanted to encourage people to choose to be fabulous regardless of their circumstances, and create the life they love! Bfabulous is now the name of my business. I had never hosted my own show before.

"I learned that courage was not the absence of fear, but the triumph over it. The brave man is not he who does not feel afraid, but he who conquers that fear." — Nelson Mandela

Relocating is another opportunity that I embarked on in 2015. During my marriage, we'd considered relocating to Charlotte, NC back in 2006. I came to the realization that just because we didn't, that didn't mean I couldn't. So I relocated from Illinois to Charlotte. There were definitely many obstacles. I started a new life with my three youngest children while my oldest continued his junior year in college in Illinois. If you'd asked me five years ago, I would have never believed that I had enough courage or strength to move out of state with my children and no job, especially with my son still there. I would have shouted "NO" at the top of my lungs!

What are some opportunities that you may have come across that caught your attention, but you really did not take the time to look into? Is there something that you are interested in that by making a few calls to certain people or organizations you might be able to find or create an opportunity? Social media has provided us with a vast networking capability. Many of us use it for social reasons, but it is a great tool to locate businesses, organizations, people, and groups where you can connect, learn valuable information, and find resources to assist you. Devote specific amounts of time each day or week towards researching information and opportunities related to your goals. Get focused and purposeful about implementing what you want to do, and I believe the doors of opportunity will open for you. Please make a commitment to start the work today.

Hopefully these steps have provided you with some takeaways to be bold and walk courageously towards your dreams! Are you ready? You, reading this right now, it is time to "Live Your Best Life & Answer the Call." Yes, you, it is time do you, boo! The sky is the limit! Being happy with your life and living your purpose is the ultimate satisfaction. Each day is a blessing; share the gifts you have been given. You have all of the tools that you need inside you or within your reach to create your best life. I'm excited for you as you redesign your most beautiful artwork, you. You are a one-of-a-kind masterpiece. I am believing God's best for you, and that He will show up and show out in all areas of your life.

I look forward to helping you and hearing about your amazing stories on your journey to Bfabulous and create the life you love! Please reach out to me on social media for any speaking engagements, workshops, seminars, retreats, or coaching needs. Turn it up, shine bright, and Bfabulous!

Angie Hodges

Angie Hodges is the mom of four amazing kids, a transformational speaker, vision board and destiny workshop facilitator, coach, and now an author. Previously, she hosted her own radio show, Bfabulous on the gospel internet station SOAR Radio and is a member of the Black Belt Speaker family. She has a Bachelor's in Communications Management. Angie has developed curriculum and provided training in corporate and nonprofit settings, acted as Mistress of Ceremonies for community events, and done voiceover work as well. Born and raised in Milwaukee, Wisconsin, she relocated to Poplar Grove, Illinois and now currently resides in Charlotte, North Carolina.

Going through her own life changing experiences and challenges was the catalyst that propelled Angie on her journey of rediscovery. She has a heart for hurting people, especially woman, and vowed to God help those seeking a new direction in their lives. Angie has experience interacting with all types of general audiences as well as those specifically geared towards women, parents, and teens. She will work with you to customize a transformational encounter.

As a change expert, she specializes in helping people break free of anything that is preventing them from being the best version of themselves. In her vision board and destiny workshops, she will empower you with the tools to transform, recreate, and redefine YOU. Embrace the season you are in. Regardless of if you are single, married, widowed, a stay at home mom, a professional, an empty nester, retired, engaged… Bfabulous and live the life you love!

If you need an engaging motivational speaker for your corporation, organization, women's group, or empowerment retreat, reach out to me today!

You can reach Angie at:
Email: angie.hodges@outlook.com
Instagram: Bfabulous01
Facebook Fan Page: Bfabulous

Peace & Blessings!

We Are Inadequate... Aren't We?
Cori Briggs

"Our deepest fear is not that we are inadequate. Our deepest fear is that we are powerful beyond measure. It is our light, not our darkness that most frightens us. Your playing small does not serve the world."
— Marianne Williamson

Life in and of itself is filled with a multitude of decisions! It's documented that the average adult makes roughly 35,000 decisions a day — in contrast, most children make about 3,000. Our lives can be altered in a split second, because it's predicated on our decisions. Often, our decisions are made in response to being asked a question. I often think about the toughest question I was asked, as well as my answer. However, because I was a child at the time of being asked, did I really have a choice in the decision? Did I really have an impact in the outcome of the situation that led to me being posed the question that I faced?

It all started at 5:06 a.m. at Washington Hospital Center in Washington, D.C. on March 28, 1979. Charles and Ethel Briggs gave birth to a baby boy! A baby boy that would turn out to be their only son, and their only child. Our young family lived in the inner city for a couple of years before moving directly outside of the city to District Heights, Maryland. From my childhood perspective, all seemed to be well. I'm sure that for all of us, there are various moments that stand out when we think about our childhood. I can say that from what I can remember, everything was great!

Phenomenal birthdays filled with comic-themed parties, down to my pops making cheese toast covered with cinnamon and sugar, partnered with the perfect cup of strawberry milk as we headed to the Early Learning Center. I even remember holding onto my Nuk pacifier as I walked into school, slipping it into my father's jacket pocket before any of my classmates had a chance to see me. Life was great! I mean, really great — aside from having to monitor my beverage intake to close to bed. Come on now, you know what I'm talking about.

As I got older, I remember riding shotgun with my mother as we weaved our way through D.C. rush-hour traffic as she headed to work. I'd be dropped off at my elementary school, where the principal was a really close friend of the family, so close that I knew him as my uncle. Principal or not, he was super cool. It didn't matter if I was running by him in my parent's basement at one of the infamous card parties where the lines were drawn on the Pinochle tables, or passing by him in the hall and no other students were around. He would always say, "What's up, Co-G!?" It was short for my first and middle name's put together. He made me feel like I was the man! In addition to their immense love, my parents surrounded me with a close village of their friends, who had a vested interest in seeing me grow and shine. Even if it wasn't actually the case I didn't think it — I knew with confidence that I was special. I can't help but smile when I think about how much love was poured into me, as well as the love that surrounded me.

Growing up, one of my strongest inclinations was needing to toughen up as a young man. Without having any siblings and all of my cousins several hours away, where would I find my youthful toughness? I will never forget getting involved with martial arts — a large part in thanks to one of my aunts. Beyond our parents, the adults allowed in our lives have a huge impact on us, which could either be positive or negative. My martial arts instructor made a great impact on me as he pushed and pushed me to work through fear and tears no matter what. He poured into my fabric of self-confidence and taught me what it truly meant to stand up for myself.

Whether it was Uncle Bob's calm coolness I desired to emulate, or the gritty attitude and high-flying tornado kicks of my martial arts instructor, absolutely nothing could have prepared me for that question. That question that came barreling at me like a freight train out of a tunnel, only this tunnel was in my parents' bedroom. Well, what once was their bedroom. At one point, they were living across a small hall from each other, each in their own room. On this particular day, however, they were in their room together. The bed was topped by the Sunday comics, as my pops never missed his newspaper read. I don't really remember verbatim what was said, but the question was asked something like this: *"So if you had to pick one of us to live with, which would it be?"*

What did they just ask me? With just eight years of life under my belt, did they just ask me if I had to choose one of them to live with, who would it be? This isn't real, is it?

Did this come from out of one of the comic strips I recall looking back at me? How do I make this decision? I loved them both so very much — I wanted to live with both of them. The silence and small pause after the question seemed like it went on forever. With my childhood sense of wisdom, I immediately thought about whose punishments were the least scary. I mean, would you have had a better idea if you were in my shoes? How life changing was my answer going to be for all of us?

Looking back, the exact timeline was a bit of a blur. I remember going to look at houses with my mother and one of her friends. Of course, none the wiser, I just assumed we were looking for a new house for all three of us. Talk about tough questions and tough decisions! There is nothing like being a child, awakening from a bad dream and running down the hall and having to decide whose room to run to. However, with the change that was upon us, it wasn't a matter of deciding whose room do I run to should I have a bad dream… there would be only one room to run to, where I will only find one parent.

As I've gotten older and experienced more of life, I have learned that when we have experiences and pains that we haven't dealt with properly, we all have a tendency to go back to the very same age we were when we were wounded when we face other experiences in life that scratch at that pain or even dare to hint at that pain. I say this, knowing now that I emotionally went to back to being eight years old for a long time. I didn't even know that's what I was doing. I emotionally reverted, especially when someone would ask, "What's wrong?"

The move was a blur. I'm quite sure many things took place when I wasn't home, either at school or with a babysitter. There are a few things, though, that seemed almost as if they were in slow motion and are extremely clear to me. One such instance was the very moment we moved into the new house. Without any communication or warning from my mother, we had company. I guess it's better to say my mother had company — a man, large in stature and presence, with an extremely engaging personality. What's crazy was that this wasn't my first time seeing him. However, I never thought from that day forward that I'd be seeing him for the rest of my life! I remember his entrance and his impressionable footsteps on each stair as he walked up the steps where he met my mother in the kitchen, and I was left alone downstairs, only wonder, who is this and why is he here? Had I created this outcome with my answer? I was left confused, scared, worried, and with ton of unanswered questions. I wasn't short on any love — on the next day and those to follow, my mother's interactions with me were normal. You would think it was any other day! It was not as if we hadn't just moved thirty minutes away and had someone come visit us at our new house, which was probably the latest I recall us ever having visitors.

As time passed, it was clear that my mother had a new relationship — a new companion in her life to replace the role for her that had been my father's. Again, this was gathered through common sense and deductive reasoning as an every-other-night visit turned into every night. At first, he would be gone before I was up and getting ready for school the next morning. Then we were jockeying to see who got to the bathroom first because you could very well say we shared it. It wasn't just my toothbrush in the bathroom anymore, and I hadn't started shaving or wearing deodorant yet. We all lived together — he, my mother, and I. I wasn't asked any more questions. Maybe, at least as far as my mother was concerned, I had said it all in that one answer.

Following the move, what seemed to be new and exciting times for my mother seemed to be the very exact opposite for my father. There weren't any more "family meetings" with the Sunday funnies laid out in my "parents' room." It was obvious it would never, ever be the same again. I will never forget Saturdays, because that's when my pops came to pick me up. Typically, it was by about 10 a.m. or so. I would be with my mother at her house during the week, then at my pop's house on the weekends. Time is truly our most valuable asset. Looking back, it's pretty interesting how my pops let me have my time. When I made the decision to move with my mother, I never thought about moving away from the neighborhood friends that I had been growing up with. Not to mention moving into a neighborhood where a lot of the neighbors didn't look like us, nor were we close in age. At the time, I never wondered how it may be possible for me to almost hop out of the car before he even stopped and parked in the driveway as we pulled up to his house as I was itching to get outside. Saturday was my day to go outside and find a way to play with friends. Isn't that what all children did on Saturday afternoons?

Even with the forfeiture of the time, my pops always looked for ways for he and I to talk. Although I could really tell he was far less happy with things than my mother, he never said anything negative about my mother or her new companion. I will never ever forget my pops dropping me off and placing the car in park in my mother's driveway and looking me in my eyes, saying, "Son, please know another man will never raise you. Another man will not raise my son!" This statement would be one of the most powerful things my father would ever say to me. He'd always write letters to my mother on yellow legal pads, and he'd fold a check inside the page. Most Sundays, when dropping me off, he'd walk me to the door and hand the letter and check to my mother. On other occasions, he would give clear directions to make sure I placed it in her hand as soon as I walked in the house.

Revisiting this time of my life impacted me in a lot of ways. When it all began, I was several years away from adolescence and had not begun to decipher life through my own eyes and heart. As I got older, my lack of communication with my mother about matters of the heart — both hers and my own — created frustration and anger. My immaturity and lack of overall understanding caused me to direct those hurt feelings and anger at my father for allowing this to happen to us. Like most children, I'm sure at some point there was the wonder of why, how, and when. Why was this happening? Though I didn't want for anything material, it's safe to say I was spoiled a little. I had what I needed and, more often than not, what I wanted, materially. How did this happen? And as far as when... Well, it all started when I was asked that question as far as I was concerned. I would have given anything for there to be a reset button. Even if that wasn't possible, I would have traded a pair or two pairs or more of sneakers for us all to be in the same house again. I would've traded them to have a real conversation with my mother about my heart and feelings because I knew that would happen before we'd ever been all under the same roof. I would've traded anything and then some to know what was really being exchanged via those old yellow legal pages other than a check.

Through this experience, I was always given plenty of love and support from both of my parents in my academics as well as those things I expressed interest in outside of the classroom. Those interests mainly surrounded athletics, and football was my first love. Signals were mixed at times from my parents. Early on, my father didn't approve of me playing football because he didn't want me to get hurt. Yet, after the move, my mom allowed me to play, thinking that I'd shy away from the very first bit of contact, but to her surprise, I fell in love. Athletics and friendships became my escape — they became my opportunity not to sit in my feelings and simply be consumed in them all the time. Athletically, I became a jack of all that I played, but I didn't allow myself to master one. This, again, is where I can say there were mixed signals from my point of view. It was the push for me to be active versus more of what I would truly get out of committing to one. However, I loved it! From one season to the next, as the game and ball changed, so did I. Mediocrity set in, as I also did just enough in the classroom so my parents wouldn't fuss too much and I could keep playing whatever it was I was playing at the time — especially during football season.

My parents' divorce, along with being the only child, caused me to also over-inflate the value of my relationships. As I began to date, I gave the relationships and the young ladies too much, too fast. I didn't want to be like my parents. So instead of dating, I engaged as if I was in little mini-marriages, which probably made me a turn off over time. I say this as in reflecting on my first so called "serious relationships" of dating, which always resulted in my getting dumped. I couldn't believe it, but I was the one being told that the relationship was to be no more. I also clung to my friendships, only to have things come to a head my junior year of high school. I will never forget being ditched by the two guys who were supposedly the closest two friends I had at the time. I vividly recall talking on the phone daily and hanging together that summer up until the two of them were walking down the school hall that next school year. It was just the three of us in the hall, and it was as if I wasn't even there. Talk about devastating. This was the straw that broke the camel's back! I was a walking powder keg of pent-up anger and frustration. I seemed to be happy on the outside, but I was a ball of negative energy and emotion on the inside.

For the longest time, I convinced myself that the reason I didn't create the stir I should've my senior year playing football was because I just got hurt. I remember it like it was yesterday. It was the first Friday night game of the season as we typically played on Saturdays. It had rained that day, so the ground was wet and slippery. Thinking I was making the most logical decision, I switched out my cleats for some longer ones. I was listening with great intent in the huddle to fulfill my assignment on each play. However, the next play's call would result in those longer cleats doing their job, with me planting my foot in the ground only to have it not give when I needed it to, and I suffered a severe ankle sprain of all the major ligaments. What hurt even more than the injury was my choosing to sit out my junior year and not play, despite even being asked by the head coach. I was just angry! I was so frustrated with things, and I hurt myself even more by putting down my favorite sport. I chose not to play a game that had been my everything since the fourth grade. All the work and consistency in playing had been for that very moment. However, in the midst of overwhelming emotions, I squandered a large and great opportunity.

Even though I was committed to my athletics and fought hard to get back on the field as soon as possible during my senior year following my injury, I found time to begin to experiment with smoking and drinking, looking to escape or using it as a means to cope. Emotionally, the heaviness of my parents' and our family's separation continued to weigh me down and create more frustration with me. During this time, I began driving, and I started to slowly but surely make it my business to move in with my father. Seemingly against his wishes, and definitely against my mother's, but I was the one driving myself back and forth between their houses, so it wasn't something that was easy for them to stop, even if they wanted to. Though we never really spoke about it, I really think my father didn't want to create a negative wave with my mother. Despite all that had been, I knew in my mother's heart, she simply didn't want to be without me. One thing is for certain — I walked through life with a "me against the world" attitude.

From the moment I was asked who I'd choose to live with, I'd wondered if I'd done something to cause this — if it was all my fault. Although I felt like we were best friends at times, I'd stuffed down a lot of feelings, which made me question my mother's love for me. I wondered why my mother had decided to put someone else before me. Being a child, I wondered — was my father truly a real man because this had happened? Things were very challenging and I didn't feel confident in knowing who I was. Although I did my best to convince others, and even more so myself, that I wasn't average, a large majority of my actions were just that — average. I placed so much emphasis into being different, but I still was average.

I've learned that each of us tends to feel like our situation is the most devastating thing in the world because it's ours. With a divorce rate of 50% in the United States alone, I'm sure several readers may have had similar experiences to mine, or maybe even worse. Similar is just that — *similar* — not exactly the same. It's quite possible your experience may have involved parents who were never married, or a situation where one of your parents simply wasn't present at all. There is one thing we all have in common, no matter what the experiences we've faced. What we see in or didn't see in our parents sets the early foundation for how we all will enter relationships with others. Friends, romantic partners, but even more, ourselves!

There is so much more to this story — my story. Looking back, I found myself maintaining through my relationships with others, with the fellas as well as my girlfriends. A good deal of my energy was put into fulfilling my dream as a top high-school recruit, then onto college, playing my favorite sport at a high level. However, when I truly reflect, it was my relationships, especially with my girlfriends, that filled my time when I wasn't in practice or in a game. That dreadful junior year of high school really became my internal tipping point, as I was consumed by my own hurt, pain, and frustration of what had been out of my control with my parents. My girlfriend's mother became a huge outlet source, as she really allowed and encouraged me to communicate feelings I had that I don't think I ever articulated to anyone or even admitted to myself. My relationship with my girlfriend's mother was unique as she was a lot younger than other parents, and she took the time to relate to me, which allowed me to put my guard down and open up. As the majority of high school relationships tend to run their course, so did this one for me. However, her mother and I maintained a friendly relationship for a good while to follow.

I also didn't recognize the great value I received from the gentleman who was my mother's companion for so long. He made a great impression on me as a sound voice of reason, directly and indirectly, as he was clear to not attempt to cause my father nor me to feel like he was stepping on anyone's toes.

As I'm pouring out, it's more and more lucid to me my journey was truly just beginning. It is often said that we never know what we have until it is gone. The journey that was mine didn't begin to have vision until I left home. It was at that time I was to be with myself that true clarity all started...

We Are Powerful Beyond Measure
Cori Briggs

"There is nothing enlightened about shrinking so that other people won't feel insecure around you. We are all meant to shine as children do. It's not just in some of us; it's in everyone. And as we let our light shine, we unconsciously give other people permission to do the same. As we are liberated from our own fear, our presence automatically liberates others." — Marianne Williamson

We are all truly powerful beyond measure, but do we really know it? My personal journey was laced with challenges that created multiple layers of self-imposed limitations. Limitations that got in my way, and did so quite often. Or, better said, limitations that I allowed to get in my way! The greatest challenge was that I didn't even know how to articulate or where to begin the process of overcoming those limitations. My point of acceptance was years in the making. However, with certain seeds of positivity sown, unbeknownst to me, once water hit those seeds, they had no choice but to grow.

Oftentimes, many of us are unable to obtain clarity due to the numerous distractions around us every day. Better yet — some of us are afraid to let go of the very thing or things we are clinging to that are stifling us from answering our call in this life. It was clear to me before being able to even hear my calling that the anger and the frustration that engulfed me had to be removed. There was also a large part of me that needed to heal.

The influence of a higher power has tremendous impact on who people are, what they learn, and who they know themselves to be. In both my grandparents and my parents, I saw consistent religious practices. However, it wasn't until I grew older that I really understood the difference in someone being very religious and someone being very spiritual. I also discovered that being in tune with your spiritual self is okay, and an essential component of learning who you truly are. Connecting internally and spiritually is sincerely knowing who you are at the core — deep down inside. Knowing how to answer the calling on your life has its foundation in knowing your true, inner, spiritual self. I write the following with respect for you as a reader, knowing that religion and spirituality can be very sensitive. I'm certain that you can be empowered and healed, just as I was. Regardless of what my parents and their parents felt and had for themselves, I needed to discover my own spiritual self and create my own spiritual relationship with The Source.

Truly learning how to love myself started once I fully committed to my personal spiritual walk. All love in life begins with that love of self. Our spiritual connections keep us in line and in tune with this vital piece of personal existence. I've learned that when we make time to pray, we communicate to the Most High. When we create time and space to meditate, this allows the Most High to communicate to us. As we make decisions, address life's questions, and search for answers, our spiritual grounding provides us with the necessary stability and guidance. Having a strong and solid spiritual connection allows us to do this and know we are never walking in this life alone. Sharing love in life is powerful! A good bit of my anger stemmed from questioning how loved I was in response to what happened to our family and us no longer physically being together anymore.

Though it wasn't about me, I had to learn the feelings I did have were a by-product of what my parents were going through at the time. Of course, there were other experiences that impacted me, but they all grew out of this initial incident. As I began to sincerely learn my spiritual self, it allowed me to honestly see that nothing in the world compromised my connection to my Creator and the power of spiritual love. Being able to love myself and know the power of divine love allowed me to genuinely be able to love others. Learning this was invaluable in my continuing to grow and heal, as well as really, really become my authentic self. This created the environment for real healing to begin. Parts of my heart that I didn't even know needed healing began to do so. My spiritual connection and alignment taught me how to navigate my emotional self and what impacted me inside, both negatively and positively. In this, the healing process was really able to take shape and allow me to open up myself from inside out.

Being able to answer our individual call in life starts with knowing who we are spiritually. Having a connection to the spiritual force within us tallows us to be able to create and manifest that which is inside of each of us. When we work in one accord with our higher power, we have the ability to manifest our dreams. Our spiritual connection reiterates and establishes our true worth and value to the entire world — a value and worth not to be defined by others. This is one of the most empowering experiences for us to have. Knowing your value and what it is you have been given to offer and share with the world is liberation within itself. Following your spiritual connection and growth is critical in continuing forward and upward progress in life. I not only had to forgive my parents (as they did their very best), I had to learn to forgive myself. I surely wasn't the model son, especially as I got older.

For most of us, real forgiveness is a large mountain to climb. It can be a lot easier to *say* that you forgive than actually, sincerely forgiving someone and even more, forgiving yourself. True forgiveness promotes peace and balance. Before I could reach a place of growth and see myself for what I was at my core, I first had to learn to forgive. As I came into alignment with my spiritual self, my increasing spirituality enveloped the power that forgiveness has. My learning and maturing made me recognize that real credibility had to be extended to my parents — before they were my parents or anything else on this planet, they were simply human. Without a doubt, both of them have and still would give their all to see me have the very best that life has to offer. In turn, I had to learn the importance of forgiving myself! I realized that some of the negative energy that I carried around inside of me was from me being angry and upset with Cori. A lot of us will be harder on ourselves than we are on others, and harder on ourselves than others are on us. I finally had to allow myself to accept that there was a necessity for me to just let go of certain things. Some of what had occurred was beyond my control. Because of my emotional state as well as emotional IQ, I didn't maximize some of the greatest opportunities that my life had to offer that were right there in front of me. Opportunities I was afforded because of my parents, despite ultimately what was *their* situation. Forgiveness of self is vital to overcoming life's obstacles and challenges.

Who are we at our core? What is our true fabric of makes us who we really are from the inside out? Many of us look to deny our experiences in life because of the pain they caused. Many of us want to simply forget about it because of the impact it made on our hearts and emotions. We cannot and should not deny our experiences, because they make us who we are. We allow those experiences to create emotional, spiritual, and physical growth, or sheer destruction along with self-limitation. Each of us must make a commitment to our own personal growth and development. For me, beginning to learn to invest in myself was invaluable! Who are we with ourselves? Who are we to those we interact with? Without commitment to ongoing growth, there is no way — even if one knows their calling in life — that they can really cultivate and nourish it so it grows inside them and outside of them abundantly. Personal development is a lifelong, ongoing process and a journey that must be valued, appreciated, and cultivated.

When it began for me, I couldn't get enough of books like this very one you're reading right now, and any that I could get my hands on that would challenge me internally. I searched for material and information that would guide me in the direction of programming my gifts and imagination, which were given to me and only me. They also helped me reprogram various pieces of myself where poor decisions or responses to experiences had created a negative impact. Each of us must take ownership in knowing we aren't perfect! We have made some mistakes that require us to be accountable and reprogram certain aspects of who we are. Our personal development and growth is just that — personal. It allows us the opportunity to assess our strengths and skills. Personal development allows us to assess our special something that separates us from others, and then reflect and consider our aims and goals in life. That's when we began to see our inner light through our aims and goals we've set. As we work towards them, we're able to truly realize and maximize our fullest potential. I feel I am still embracing and pouring into this because it is indeed a journey. It is a process of life! Do you have someone traveling your personal development and growth journey with you? Though many of us think we can, no one travels through life and is able to truly grow without the help of someone or a group of people along the way.

Each of us can lay out the most masterful plan. However, without putting that plan into action, without putting it into its implementation phase, it's just that — a plan. Many fail to take action because we are awaiting the perfect plan. We create other obstacles for ourselves through overthinking or simply attempting to rationalize every single detail before we actually move forward. Oftentimes, we don't see that without enacting and creating action, what we are ultimately looking for won't occur. The creation of action creates more action. As we formulate our plans, the next steps often aren't actualized until the initial actions takes place. With firm conviction, I've learned firsthand that for anyone to answer their call, they must take action!

All of us need to overcome our life's obstacles and fully embrace what it is we've been called to do. I mean the true knowing of what we were each placed on this earth and called to do — our purpose. While growing through my childhood into adolescence and even into young adulthood, I had to realize conquering the challenges within was the key to my ultimate growth. I am confident in sharing those steps to aid and guide you. Without them, I would have never been in position to wholeheartedly answer my call. May the following four milestones contribute to you unlocking the call within that is to be answered by you and only you.

1. Getting Connected with One's Spiritual Self

We must find and define our spiritual selves to completely be whole. It was in my spirituality that I could truly be honest with myself. Gaining spiritual insight placed me in a position to be completely open and vulnerable, free from any judgment.

Growing spiritually allows us to learn the value of our best self and eliminate questions surrounding our existence. When we solidify our connection to our spiritual source, how we approach decisions and answer life's questions changes for the better. With strength in our spiritual connection, we realize we are no longer alone in this life. We are all divinely created. In us finding our spiritual selves, we can embrace the guidance bestowed upon us and truly know who we are versus simply just only having the possible belief of what we've been told. By embracing and harnessing that spirit inside, we can manifest those things around us and in our lives. A strong spiritual self and understanding leads to a well-developed emotional IQ. When properly exercised on a regular basis, we are better prepared to navigate our life's experiences, both positive and negative. In our spiritual growth, we remove any limiting beliefs that have stifled our growth. In our spiritual strength, we can see and feel how strong we truly are as beings, and that the only limits we have are the ones we place on ourselves. There is no love like that of spiritual love! Through this divine love, we are filled with a love powerful enough that we become the love that is in us, and are feely willing to share it as a love of a higher power loves us. Ultimately, with your spiritual foundation, you are thoroughly rooted in knowing who you are and are not to be easily moved by others or deterred from your inner peace and relationship with your Source, synching you to your life and its purpose.

2. Implore the Selfless Act of Forgiveness

This requires truthfully not only forgiving others whom may have impacted us negatively or hurt us, but real forgiveness of self. Real forgiveness is real freedom! We waste so much energy on others when we control so much of freedom and happiness internally. Forgiveness provides the inner most healing truly necessary in conquering pain, and oftentimes, bitterness as well as anger. Within true forgiveness, we find and establish healing. Because of its genuineness, forgiveness is heavily linked to the very first step of spiritual connection. Forgiveness is so powerful in its impact because in order for it to happen, one must do so consciously. Because of this consciousness, it acts as a natural catalyst to eliminate bouts with anxiety, internal and external relationship conflicts, and even depression. When I reflect on what caused my frustration and anger, depression was present, and I didn't even know it. However, true forgiveness creates the platform for strong emotions that are charged with negativity to be released. This creates a new atmosphere of positivity, love, and happiness.

3. The Greatest Investment is Self-Investment

Personal development is your foundation of empowerment. It's a lifelong process of assessing and reassessing our skills and strengths, and then utilizing that continuous assessment to maximize our fullest potential. When we truly feel empowered in life, we begin to adjust our perspective and seek out ways to maximize that which is inside of us. Once we truly begin to develop and feel good about ourselves, it creates an ease where others feel good about us, too. By investing in self, you learn how to fully manage you! You learn how to be best prepared in life and adapt in navigating your life and what it has to offer. At its core, personal development begins with learning one's true self and value system. This is so vital in knowing what our purpose is. The emphasis on personal development elevates inspiration for us to pursue what we find to be the most fulfilling in life.

4. All Things Require A.C.T.I.O.N.

The most vital step of them all — taking A.C.T.I.O.N.! Why is this the most vital and critical step? It's because all things, including this process, begin with your actions. It's time! The time is and has been now! In order for any of the steps we take to mean something, taking A.C.T.I.O.N. is imperative. Action was necessary in starting my personal journey, as it will be for you. Too many times, we all fail to do certain things because of false limits we surround ourselves with. What happens when those fallacies are removed and we are ready to act? The possibilities are endless. Everyone on the entire earth could write at least one book. If that is so true, then why don't more people do it? Everyone thinks of a million-dollar idea once or even twice a year. Why is it they don't act on it and follow through? Too many people are afraid and fail to realize action is an extremely vital piece of the life fulfillment equation. The beginning to anything starts with A.C.T.I.O.N.!

Our ability to not only find our purpose, but then to completely answer the call placed upon us starts with action. Are you ready to answer your call? Are you ready to fulfill your assignment? Maybe you don't quite know what that is yet, and that's okay. It is just like a telephone ringing — if you don't stop what you are doing and make time to actually pick up the phone and accept the call, it will ring and ring and ring, going unanswered.

Keys to Answering the Call

1) Getting Connected with One's Spiritual Self
2) Implore the Selfless Act of Forgiveness
3) The Greatest Investment is Self-Investment
4) All Things Require A.C.T.I.O.N.

I have learned that my true calling and purpose is to inspire, impact, and aid others in their personal transformation journey. After fourteen years of both corporate and entrepreneurial experience, I really began to see my value was to truly tap into people and guide them in seeing their true self. One of the most valuable components in discovering my calling came by way of my marriage and being a parent. Because of the vulnerability required to be successful within a marriage, my wife has been indispensable in uncovering the gift within me to answer my life's call. Besides my loving marriage, being a father has been key in knowing my call was to be answered. It's critical that my daughter see me live by the same values and principles my wife and I communicate to instill in her daily as being necessary for her to live her life to the fullest! I learned that we all must share our gifts, as I'm sharing with you right now. We never know who we are intended to impact based on answering our call. We grow through what we go through for other people, based on our life's assignment. In answering my call, I'm focused and committed to assisting in the transformation of individual's lives around the entire world.

Please know that this body of work you are reading is only possible with action. Did I ever hesitate? Yes, of course I did! Was I ever scared or fearful? Yes! However, I was even more afraid and fearful of not taking a step. I was more afraid and fearful of what it would be like to have never put this into words with pen to paper. I was more afraid to see what the outcome would be of *not* answering my call.

What it would look like to not have stepped into my purpose drives me on a daily basis? Action is indeed everything! Action allows someone to definitively step into who they are intended to be. Action allows you to do this even if you don't know all the steps and intricate details to get it done. Oddly enough, you won't know until you commit to acting. That's the part of the journey of answering your call. In order for you and me both to learn, grow, and develop our calling to know what's next, we must simply start and take action. Imperfect actions are far superior to taking no actions at all. By choosing not to fully use what was divinely placed in us, or execute with what it was that we were given, we are not living our lives to the fullest. Our greatest gifts were given to us and placed within us to be used. The great artist Pablo Picasso said, "The meaning of life is to find our gift, then the purpose of life is to give it away."

Our lives, to me, can be defined essentially by our will. By definition, "will" is something to be expressed in the future tense. Will is the expression of inevitable events, or someone expressing a request, desire, consent, or willingness to do something. Will is the expression of facts about an individual's ability or capacity. When we express a habitual behavior, it is our will. When we choose to express the probabilities or the expectations of those things that are to occur in the present, it is will. Right now, in this very moment as you are reading, I know with conviction this is my will. I see that with my gift of inspiring others it is my God-given will to touch, impact, transform, and change lives.

Each of us is on this journey we know and call life. I am fully committed to my own journey, and it does indeed involve you. It involves you, should you allow me to be that someone to aid and assist in your transformation to maximize the gift and greatness inside of you. Please be my guest and connect with me on Facebook. I would love to have you join our Facebook Group – The Builder's Legion. This is our online community of individuals looking for a place of positive energy, revitalization, and inspiration. Be sure to visit my website, corigbriggs.com, as well. Let's build together on our journeys, and allow me to walk with you toward your limitless results within a limitless life. Allow me to provide a charge for you along your path of discovering and defining your life's purpose! Then, in turn, how you can answer your call and give that gift away! If you will, I will, we will — Let's Build!

Cori G. Briggs

Cori G. Briggs is a native of the nation's capital who grew up in District Heights, Maryland. He is a graduate of Florida Agricultural & Mechanical University who studied business administration as well as psychology.

Cori is a devoted family man. He is married to his beautiful wife, Kandyce, and is the proud father of his lovely daughter, Haile. He stands firm that we should operate with our last names first, keeping in mind the importance of creating our legacies.

With 14 years of leadership training, development, management, and entrepreneurial experience, he utilizes this to enrich others on their journey to find and tap into their Gift. Cori pursues his purpose by building leaders to build other leaders while inspiring personal growth and financial empowerment.

Website: corigbriggs.com
Email: thebuilder@corigbriggs.com

Roller Coaster of Pain
Rosetta West

"Pain is a physical and emotional experience that impacts every aspect of a person's life."
— Dr. Stephen Thorp

The physical and emotional pain was pushing toward a ride I did not want to go on. What I did not know was that I had a call to answer, and preparations were being made.

I was born in March of 1950; by the year of 1956, a pain journey had started in my life. The memory of waking up crying because of the pain in my legs and arms is still real. The doctor informed my parents the pain was the result of growing so fast, and at twelve years of age, I would outgrow it. In the meanwhile, Grandmother Mumsie said to Mom and Dad, "Place warm bricks in the oven, wrap a thick towel around them, and place by the limbs that are hurting." She said, "There is more to this story; just wait and see."

Dad did not need an alarm clock to wake him up for work because he was usually up already, warming and wrapping bricks, making me comfortable before he left for work. Unfortunately, the doctor was wrong — things did not change for me when I turned 12. The pain I experienced starting at six is still with me today.

"To wish to be well is a part of becoming well."
— Seneca

Growing up, I did not like amusement park rides, especially the roller coasters. However, I found myself on one, and not by choice. I did not go to an amusement park to get on it. This was a roller coaster of emotional pain, found inside of the body — heart, mind, and whole being. The Bible says in Proverbs 4:23, "Above all else, guard the heart, for everything was done flows from it."

This emotional roller coaster of pain that was running too fast, out of control, and I wanted off. By 1962, there were six boys and four girls, and before long there would be two more, making twelve children in our family.

I accepted Christ as my personal savior at the age of nine. We were doing church daily. Because of the limitations and restrictions put on me by the church and my parents, I begin to withdraw from participating in any part of the church. Every child should be able to watch the *Wizard of Oz* growing up, but not us. It came on television Sunday evening, a church night. The last straw was when my parents took the family to the carnival at the grade school we attended. Just so happened it was on a Friday night, which was a church night. Friday evening service started with prayer at 7:30 p.m. and evening worship service at 8:00 p.m. The carnival started at 6 p.m. and ended at 8:30 p.m. After the festival ended, we immediately went to church, which went on for at least 2-3 more hours. Our senior pastor made all the children that attended the event to kneel at the altar and tarry until he felt it was long enough, get up before the church, ask God, him, and the church to forgive us for going. From that day forward, I started to do things that were wrong and did not want to go are be part of the church anymore.

One day, a decision was made, and not a good one. A young lady in the church, who had the gift of prophecy, came 3 times with prophetic words from God. The words of rebuke, warning, and destruction fell on deaf ears. I made no amends. Whatever happened would not be that bad; broken leg or broken arm, okay; death was not acceptable, and I was just a child, that should count for something. I wanted to help my parents in any way possible. One way I chose to help was by not complaining when I didn't feel well. For three months, I had a sore throat. I tried doctoring my sore throat; it did not work. I informed the school nurse of the illness, she, in turn, made a call to my parents asking them to immediately pick up their sick daughter from school and go straight to the doctor. That is what they did. They did lab work at the physician's office. The doctor told my parents to start giving me the antibiotics, and expect a call in the early morning. At age twelve, the pain that was suffered at the beginning of my childhood still manifested itself, along with an illness not yet identified. That night, we saw my body temperature rise to 104°. By morning, I could not get out of bed. All of my body's joints had seized up, and any movement caused me to scream out in excruciating pain. The call came from the doctor, who diagnosed me with Rheumatic fever — an inflammatory disease that could involve the heart, joints, skin, and brain. It manifested from weeks of non-treatment of a streptococcal throat infection — the sore throat I wouldn't complain about. For three months, this illness ravished my entire body. The fever cooked my skin so badly that the top layer could be peeled off like the top layer of an onion. I was taking every available medication to no effect. Our church was praying, people were bringing what seemed like last suppers, and the home remedies were coming in daily. I was tired of being sick and in pain. I spoke to Dad, telling him I was ready to die and had repented of all sins. If God chose to restore my health, I would change the way I lived life. After sharing my feelings with my father, another prophecy was given to me. The prophecy was to read Psalms 50:14 -15, "Offer unto God thanksgiving, and pay thy vows unto the most High: and call upon me in the day of trouble: I will deliver thee, and thou shalt glorify me." These were words of comfort and restoration, and I was willing to fulfill the request and wait for God to restore my health. He delivered me. My love for the church was stronger, my faith was renewed, and I worked diligently wherever I was needed.

I remembered back to when I was 9, sitting in church and being asked to come up for prayer. I stood in front of the church for prayer, and heard these words: "Lord, give her perseverance." What was that? I hurried home to find that word in the dictionary. It said perseverance is steady persistence in the course of action, a purpose, or a state, especially despite difficulties, obstacles, or discouragement — continuance in a state of grace to the end.

What does that mean to a nine-year-old child? Justly put, nothing at the time. However, it is starting to say a little something today.

"You may not understand today or tomorrow, but

eventually, God will reveal why you went through everything you did."

Growing up, I loved being part of the church ministry. Our parents were devoted church members, and so were we. We were in church all the time. Our dad served in the capacity of a pastor and preacher, so we were known as a PK kids. That meant we were held to a higher standard and under a microscope. At 17, I was a high school senior, Sunday school teacher, choir directress, pianist, and a founding member of a group called Faithettes. We sang and traveled throughout Kansas, Oklahoma, Missouri, and Nebraska. In the midst of all of this, the roller coaster of pain reached another height.

Despite my desire to please God and my parents, I ended up pregnant and not married. I was in total shock. My life turned into a living hell — especially in the church. The spotlight was on me, and I was feeling alone, embarrassed, humiliated, and ostracized. The pain was intense, and emotions were high. I asked myself, "Why stay here? Is this who you are, and what you are going to settle for?"

The father of my child attended the same church, where he taught the young men's class and provided transportation to most of the members of the church. It was as if I'd gone through artificial insemination to become pregnant. I was on display, made to stand in front of the congregation to repent and ask forgiveness from the church and then God. However, even with all that, the church still treated me as if I never repented.

"The struggle you're in today is developing the strength you need for tomorrow."

    I knew God forgave me, but people of the church were still punishing me. I had contaminated their building. They put me on display with their mouths and their actions and put a different spin on "'Vengeance is mine' says the Lord"; it was "'Vengeance is ours,' says the church."

"But what we can do, as flawed as we are, is still seeing God in other people, and do our best to help them find their grace. That's what I strive to do; that's what I pray to do every day." — Barack Obama

    The pastor relieved me of all my church positions until my child was born. He informed me that there would be total restoration to these posts. That promise never came to fruition. Three months into my pregnancy, the father of my child and I were married.

"If you're walking down the right path and you're willing to keep walking, eventually, you'll make progress."
— Barack Obama

    To enter the sanctuary, I walked into the vestibule of the church where you took last-minute looks at yourself to make sure you look presentable. I could hear the teacher of the Bible Study Class, along with the students, talking and saying things not to restore me but to destroy me behind closed doors, and put on superficial acts when they were in my presence. I put on my best friendly face and walked in.

In the Bible, Ephesians 4:32 says, "And be ye kind one to another, tenderhearted, forgiving one another, even as God for Christ's sake hath forgiven you."

I forgive them!

"Take very little notice on those people who choose to treat you poorly. It is how they are defining their story, not yours." — Lei Wah

Now I understand the importance of the word "perseverance." Everything I've been through built that understanding. I realized that my life has a purpose. Doing good in life and not intentionally causing harm to others was a must for me. I strive to never judge or compare my life to someone else's. Instead, I share my life while genuinely loving and caring about others, making sure no treatment given on my watch resembled the way people had treated me. So, no excuses for who I am. I had to fight through many bad days to earn the best days of my life. However, even as a child, some things would tempt me to give up on life and people. I needed perseverance; a preservative, and I needed to persevere. With a childlike faith and words, I needed something that would keep me safe. My dad was the greatest provider and protector, yet I needed more. In the world that I was going to live in, and the things I would endure, I needed more. I needed GOD!

"Before you can inspire with emotion, you must be swamped with it yourself. Before you can move their tears, your own must flow. To convince them, you must yourself, believe." — Winston Churchill

My emotions were driven by insecurity and rejection in a place that should have been a haven. There was the fear of trying again, and wondering if I would be accepted and forgiven. Even though I spent a lot of time at the church, I had no real friends who were active members. I had no one in my corner to say, "I understand what you are going through, and you will make it." This setback made me realize that a reevaluation of *whose* I was and not *who* I was certainly was in order. A preacher's kid didn't get any special treatment. It made my life harder, because I was holding onto the negative emotional pain that was destroying me on a daily basis. It was decision time. Do I walk away, or I stand still and see what the end would be?

"Be a champion and go the distance even when your flesh is complaining." — Dr. Clarice Fluitt

Dr. Elizabeth Hartney stated emotional pain can become an addiction to some people. Overwhelmed with feelings of sadness, depression, guilt, shame, or fear, these emotions become so familiar and constant that you may feel like they're a part of you and you can't imagine life without them. When you are continually exposed to emotional pain, there are changes in the brain that produce a dependency on those feelings. And while this emotional pain can be significant and debilitating, when it continues on for a prolonged period of time, it also can end up affecting your physical health as well. In some instances, emotional pain can cause physical pain. While emotional pain is often dismissed as being less dangerous than physical pain, it is important that persistent emotional pain is taken seriously. In some cases, you may need to see a physician before emotional pain creates lasting consequences.

In my situation, a doctor was a necessity. This information really spoke to what was going on in my life at that time. I became a victim of the pain that was in my life. Hopeless, defeated, and unable to function rationally and routinely on a daily basis was the story. Many times, I recall sitting on the bathroom floor with a gun, driving to the lake to drown the pain, trips to the emergency room to get a shot because of a migraine headache, using prescribed drugs to self-medicate, and the physical pain throughout my body was debilitating. My best friends were sadness, unexpressed anger, anxiety, shame, and guilt. The things that I suffered were severe and dangerous.

Was I the first one to address this obstacle in the church? My guess was no. It made me question my calling. It forced me to wonder if I was fit to answer the call to ministry. But you see, I realize now — I had a call on my life. To answer this call, I had to fight through many bad days to earn the best days of my life.

"I am who I am today because of the choices I made yesterday." — Eleanor Roosevelt

In the Bible, Jeremiah 1:5 says, "Before I formed you in the womb I knew you, and before you were born I set you apart; I have appointed you as a prophet to the nations." Everything I would go through, GOD already knew.

Church was important to me. It was my lifeline, and I was allowing people to cut it off. I couldn't stop the pain. I wanted to dictate my journey and say enough is enough. I wanted to be in control. It was hard not to worry about those who talked behind my back, but I found out people were behind me for a reason.

"Your curses behind my back will not stop the blessings in my future." — Rosetta West

This destructive roller coaster of emotional and physical pain now was speeding down the next stretch of track. You know how in a baseball game, three strikes — you're out? I thought this next portion of this ride would strike me out for real.

In the ten years since my wedding day, I had given birth to three children — two sons, and one daughter. Life was good — a new home built from the ground up, had a brand new car, money was plentiful, and my husband and I both were working. Life was splendid, or so it seemed. My husband committed adultery; because of his actions, a son was born. How was I going to survive? I was angry. He had an affair with a woman of another race. What a slap in the face. In all honesty, I often wondered if he'd had an affair with a woman of same race as me, would it have hurt as much? Did she have something I did not possess? Going from feeling suicidal to homicidal, embarrassment to depression; I wondered if my children would fault me for their father's indiscretions. I had sessions with a Christian psychiatrist. It took me months to accept the violation made in our marriage. Realizing that the devil was going for the kill; it was time for battle. When you look at marriages today, adultery is running rampant from the pulpit to the door. It is widespread today in the body of Christ and the church is in trouble. Adultery is a sin that causes emotional pain, loss of life, and broken families, with children displaced and having to choose between parents. Statistics show over 50% of the marriages that end up in divorce are the results of infidelity and adultery. If you are married and having sexual intercourse with someone other than your spouse, it is a sin. For believers, look to the story of King David and his affair with Bathsheba. 2 Sam 11:2-27 should have taught those in leadership to watch for that strange man or woman that in pursuit of what does not belong to them. Some respected and anointed men and women of God have fallen victim to this sin, and thus, the anointing of God in their lives and homes was destroyed. There was a need for divine intervention of the Holy Spirit to restore my marriage to where I could start working through this crisis.

I was the born-again believer in our home, and my spouse was the non-believer. What he was doing was wrong, even as a non-believer; it was a choice and path he chose to take. The road to reconciliation was difficult for me. We had several conversations; my husband mentioned wanting to remain married. No, I did not respond with, "Okay honey." I said he had lost his entire mind now. My pain was speaking out loud. That was on top. One thing I will not be is non-transparent and say I handled this crisis in a Christ-like manner always, because I did not. I spoke at a healing wounds conference for ladies and while sharing, I talked about how at one point, I wanted to do a Muhammad Ali on my husband. You know — float like a butterfly and sting like a bee, or fix him a wake-up call breakfast, which is a pot of hot molasses and hot grits. My pain was significant, and the thought of forgiveness was something I wasn't ready for. My spouse should be punished, humiliated, ostracized, and he needed to feel every negative thing going on in my life. Divorce was not an opinion. According to my spouse, he wanted to remain married.

Major decisions should never be made in haste, nor out of pain and anger. However, for me, this was a "what would Jesus do?" challenge, and, "what is God's will for my life?" moment. I saw that the devil's job in my home, which was plagued by adultery, was to steal, kill, and destroy (John 10:10). If I wanted to remain in this marriage, the time to gird up the loins of my mind was now. I had to be alert and evalute things correctly.

"Wherefore gird up the loins of your mind, be sober, and hope to end for the grace that is to be brought unto you at the revelation of Jesus Christ." — 1 Peter 1:13 (KJV)

God assures us that He will be with us always, even in times of trouble. We know that rebuilding a relationship is not an easy task, for it will take investing time and effort on both sides to make it happen. Above all, it will take the grace of God to bring harmony into the home again. Based on my own experience, I needed to seek God's face. Prayer was a major necessity — I needed God to guide me as I sought out the right counselor. Talking to a close friend or loved one also helped the healing process. A total restoration was my desire. One Sunday, as I walked to the altar for prayer, my spirit was saying, "Lord, if you don't do it for me today, it won't get done." My pastor touched my forehead three times. Each time he said one word, "Peace. Peace. Peace."

I thank God for the peace that surpasses all understanding. My prayer for us as a couple is at the end of our life, the one left behind will testify for both of us. We have been through things that could have destroyed our marriage, but we were able to stand because God made a way. When our backs were against the wall, and it looked like it was over, He made a way. His will was fulfilled in our marriage. For those who have been betrayed and are still harboring un-forgiveness towards your spouse in your heart, you're also sinning against God. It is also unhealthy to your spirit, body, and soul. Trust the Lord for your marriage and your family, for He is with you to guide and see you through every step of the way. I cannot forget my spouse was in his flesh, and human. If we are still in the flesh, all humans — even we that are born again Christians — have the tendency to still commit sin. None of us is beyond temptation, and that is why we must ask God for His grace daily to deliver us from every temptation. Forgiveness is a big step in the reconciliation process, and it cannot be avoided.

Do your part, and leave the rest to the Lord. As He is working on you, He will also be working on your spouse through His Holy Spirit. In due time, He will make everything beautiful again. He will give you beauty for ashes and joy for pain, because you have decided to surrender all to Him. Well, all our children are married and doing great. I am still here, and divorce is not an option. In October of 2016, my spouse and I shared our forty-ninth wedding anniversary. 2017 will be our golden — fifty years!

> *"The emotion that can break your heart is sometimes the very one that heals it."* — Nicholas Sparks

Church people say some strange things if you are in church and have friends that are not. I stated early on I did not have a friend in church, but I had a childhood friend, Delores Winn Luna, who went to church but was not in church.

> *"A true friend reaches for your hand and touches your heart."* — Attributed to Heather Pryor

She was a PK kid also. She always encouraged me to stay in the church, telling me it was where I belonged. She was always there for me. We would talk, laugh, cry, and pray together. We maintain our friendship to this day. Forty years later, we work in church ministries together.

> *"Sometimes we need someone to simply be there. Not to fix anything or do anything in particular but just to let us feel*

we are supported and cared about."

When my husband stepped outside our marriage and had a baby with another woman, God was my guide and comforter; He gave me peace that surpassed all understanding. Here was a child that needed to be taken care of. Let's keep it real — many times, you will hear the complaint, "She's not spending all that money on the child." I did not go there with my spouse or the mother of the child. I assured the mother she would not have to worry about me mistreating their son. He was welcomed in my home, but he had to show respect, and could not call me by my first name. The judge gave us the opportunity to present a proposal so he could make a judgment in this case. I never argued with my spouse about him taking care of the child; it was our responsibility. Ah, keeping it real; yes, it was our responsibility. How I handled the situation made a difference in how my spouse responded to what we should do. We never argued about the child support. I embraced the child wholeheartedly. His mom and I have a great relationship. Her phone calls would start out with the hello, and then she would always refer to him as "our boy." I let the mother know he was welcome in our home and he would be treated just like his siblings. I became hands-on, realizing the shoe could be on the other foot. We had to go to court to set up child support. God gave me the dollar amount to offer, and I added in that we would provide medical, vision, dental, prescription, and life insurance. The judge approved the offer.

I decided to let our new son's mom know it was okay

to communicate about anything he needed that we could assist her with. We all moved forward in an amicable atmosphere. The other assurance I gave our new son's mom was that if he needs anything to always feel free to call. We moved forward with love, peace, and happiness in a situation that has destroyed many other families. To God be the glory.

"Forget what hurt you, but never forget what it taught you." — Unknown

"Therefore, since we are surrounded by such a great cloud of witnesses, let us throw off everything that hinders and the sin that so easily entangles. And let us run with perseverance the race marked out for us."
Hebrews 12:1 (NIV).

Never Let Go of Hope
Rosetta West

"Never let go of hope. One day you will see that it all has finally come together. What you have always wished for has finally come to be. You will look back and laugh at what has passed, and you will ask yourself... How did I get through all of that?" — Unknown

I was still holding on to the pain of unforgiveness. If you get cut with a knife, it can be a superficial cut or a deep wound. I was stuck in a rut of emotional pain that created a wound that hid itself deep within my feelings. No effort was made to nurture it back to a healthy state. I let it stay hidden in my emotions as a thickly seeded wound, infected and scabbed over. Out of sight, out of mind, yet hidden in my heart.

One day, a friend told me about an untrue accusation that was made against me. Now the tears were flowing again after years of thinking and feeling that I had moved past this situation. There was a realization that I needed to face. It was infected with unresolved issues that had scabbed over and needed the outer layer removed so real healing could take place from the inside out. Neither my head nor my heart was open to letting the issues go because the truth was not dealt with. I felt the only way to heal correctly was to hear an apology, so I could say, "I forgive you," and then let it go!

So, in praying to God, letting Him know that my HOPE was in HIM, I was ready to halt the pain and move forward. Matthew 7:7 says, "Ask, and it shall be given you, seek, and ye shall find: knock, and it shall be opened unto you." I was past knocking. To add some humor, I think banging and seriously stalking was what I was doing. This lady was ready to move forward and let go. But, if I never received a verbal apology, I was wrong for not forgiving anyway, and for that, I ask forgiveness now.

The Simplicity of How to Let Go

Here is a short exercise to directly experience the simplicity of how to let go. (This activity is inspired by The Sedona Method, developed by Lester Levenson.)

1. Find something that is soft and easily compressible (so it won't hurt your hand if you squeeze it) that will fit in the palm of your hand. A small rubber ball would be ideal, or you can wad up a piece of paper or cloth.

2. Turn your hand so that your palm is facing downward. Keeping your hand in that direction, pick up the object, and squeeze it as hard as you can with your fingers wrapped around it. Now, squeeze it even harder.

3. Squeeze it so hard that you feel a tightness and discomfort in your fist and forearm. Hold it that way for a minute or so. Now, open your fingers and let the object falls from your fingers.

So why do we make letting go of suffering more complicated than that? Because we identify with suffering, think it IS us, build an identity, and then give our allegiance to it. Daily, we feed this self-concept with our thoughts and our attention, infusing it with our Life Force. After a while, we become so used to it that we have almost entirely forgotten who we really are — the peaceful presence of Awareness that is aware OF the suffering.

"One of the most courageous decisions you'll ever make is to finally let go of what is hurting your heart and soul."
— Brigitte Nicole

Perhaps there was a time when you wanted to give up and just exist. So many things are tugging on you mentally, emotionally, and physically. The path of the choice that you can take presents different situations and results. Our attention is needed in many places. There are times you may have to let go of relationships that are unhealthy, jobs where your integrity is compromised, and habits that are destroying your body. We need to continue the fight for what is right and good. Keep fighting for your marriage, children, health, and do not forget to fight for yourself. Never let go of hope, and never give up on God. Remember, on this journey, it does not matter how strong you are, it does not matter how swift you run, what matters is that you persevered to the end, and that is a win.

"Hope returns when I remember one thing: the Lord's unfailing love and mercy still continue, fresh as the morning, as sure as the sunrise. The Lord is all I have, and so in Him, I put my hope." — Lamentations 3:21-24 (GNT)

Seek victory in every area of life that concerns you! If you feel like you are alone in the battles of life, you are not; we are not. If we are in the hands of God, strength will be provided when we need it. Isaiah 41:10 says, "So do not fear, for I am with you; do not be dismayed, for I am your God."

"Hope is for those with a future." — Vincent Weyerts

I am called to mentor children to live for Christ, encouraging them to master the gift God gave them while pushing them toward the calling they must answer to. My purpose and calling were discovered by watching an older mother working in the church with children between 4 to 12 years old. The children were healthy kids making bad choices. It was clear to me that I had a burden not just for the mother, but for the children also. It broke my heart to see the mother struggling with the children with no help. My first lesson on training toward my calling with youth started at home with my six brothers and five sisters. That lesson was to love each child as an individual with his or her own personality, protecting and guiding them while they become children of integrity (whole and complete). According to John Maxwell, "Integrity is not what we do as much as who we are," so when I saw an excellent opportunity to work with children with high potential not being tapped into, guess what? I knew it was my God-given time to go to work.

I am called to be a godly woman of transparency that would minister in compassion, binding the broken hearted, and a healer of wounded women everywhere. Opportunity presented itself while ministering to men in that area, also. Discovery came by the things I was going through. I felt my cup was a waterfall. It was just enough to get me where I needed to be, through the many storms of my life, while preparing to be qualified for the journey ahead. Learning was a gift even when the pain was a teacher.

"He sent his word, and healed them, and delivered them from their destructions." — Psalm 107:20

My developmental period started at the age of nine, where I was being prepared and equipped for my purpose. God used my education, environment, exposure, and experience to get the job done.

No matter what you go through, don't worry about naysayers. Recognize that you were chosen by God, and not the people. Yes, I was one of twelve children, but not one was an accident — each one of us was on purpose with a purpose, and I needed them all to make sure I got it right. My steps were ordered by God; where He sends me, I will go.

"When you walk, your steps will not be impeded; and if you run, you will not stumble. Take hold of instruction; do not let go. Guard her, for she is your life." — Proverbs 4:12-13

God created *me* to when I told the story people would hear, and see that there is a woman on this day, at this time, who is walking in His holiness and righteousness, demonstrating His heart's love and concern for His people as one who is willing to advance His kingdom and make His name great. One that will say to help be healed; I had to be healed myself. I had to recognize the wounds that I suffered, the help that was needed, that pretense would stop my progress, but transparency would move me to the next step, which helped me to be who God said I would be.

"It is not my capability, but my response to God's ability that counts." — Corrie Ten Boom

Maximize the Day
http://www.a4t.org/Stories/today.html

"Today, I will delete from my diary two days — yesterday and tomorrow. Yesterday was for learning; tomorrow will be a consequence of what I do today. Today, I will face life with the conviction that this day will never return, that it may be the last opportunity I'll have to contribute because there's no guarantee I'll see tomorrow. Today, I will be courageous enough not to let the opportunity pass me by; my only alternative will be to succeed. Today, I will invest my most valuable resource, my time, into my most important possession, the life God has given me. I'll spend each minute purposefully, making today a unique opportunity. I'll tackle each obstacle, knowing that with God's help, I can overcome it. Today, I will resist doubt and pessimism, and warm my world with a smile. I'll maintain a strong faith, expect nothing but the best, take the time to be happy, see every task as an opportunity to honor the Lord, and endeavor to leave His footprints on the hearts of those I meet."

Obstacles can't stop you. Problems can't stop you. Other people can't stop you. Only you can stop you.

AUTHENTIC is the word I have chosen to describe my message of my life, which is defined as a quality of being genuine and worthy of belief. I am living my best life, and I'm playing to win.

Able to speak
Unselfishly telling
Transparent stories
Heartbreaking, life changing
Experiences that
Navigate toward a
Triumphant end, producing
Inspiring results so people can look and say,
Change has come, I didn't give up, the ball is in my court, and I'm playing to win.

Here are five ways to get started creating authentic living:

1. Refine your values to know what you value and desire
2. Reevaluate and align your actions around those things
3. Be clear on what you care about
4. Promote an open mind
5. Challenge yourself to be open

Rosetta M. West

Rosetta M. West was born and raised in Topeka, Kansas. She is one of twelve children, married, and the mother of 3 children.

In 1970, I started working for Adams Business Forms, a division of Cardinal Brands. While working for them, another co-worker filed a law suit against company and union stating women were hired in at lesser pay training and doing same work as men, and that they discriminated against woman in job promotions. The lawsuit was settled in our favor in 1972. During my 38 years, because of my perseverance, I held every position from the lowest paid position to the highest paid position in the union; a working foreperson (which was a supervisor's position).

I served as the Chief Shop Steward, Union Contract Negotiator, Department Representative, and a member of Local GCIU S-580 and GCIU Local 49.

I have been a dedicated church worker and mentor to boys and girls for over fifty years in the church. In 1998 as Youth Pastor, I organized a youth ministry called Kids for Christ/Learning Links. My goal in this ministry was to nurture boys and girls by meeting them on their turf, reaching out, showing love, and connecting with all youth as they grew and discovered. The things that would help them be positive influences in their homes, schools, community, and church. These things were accomplished by showing them unconditional love, being good role models in deeds and words, helping them without compromising our goals, remaining constantly open and honest in our lifestyle, and providing opportunities for them to invite Christ into their lives as their personal savior.

I have served as: State SSB President Kansas Central Jurisdiction, SSB President at Faith Temple Church and El Shaddai Ministries, and Youth Pastor ESMCC. I now serve as Associate Pastor at ESMCC International SSB Goodwill Ambassador for the COGIC worldwide, COGIC International SSB Marshal.

Hold On — Pain Ends
Make some changes in your life!

Faith Over Fear
Anana Phifer-Derilhomme

"The journey of life can be so unpredictable, but refuse to give up, stepping onto a brand-new path will lead to brighter horizons." — Unknown

Being good held me back from answering my calling. My good paying job was sucking the very life out of me. I was waking up and doing the same thing day in and day out. I dreaded going to work every Monday. Once Sunday afternoon arrived, I was sad. I lived for the weekend and a day off. I drudged through the work week.

Being good was keeping me from being great. My "good job" was hindering me from answering the call and being all that God had called me to be. Oftentimes, we stay too long in a situation, relationship, or a community when our time or season has expired.

The day I measured up the courage and relied on my faith to contact my human resources vice president was the day I will never forget. I sat in her waiting room nervous, sad, and elated. You see, I knew this day would come. However, I didn't know how it would end. I was so unsure of the response, of the stigma that may follow me after resigning from a nationally recognized University Academic Medical Center — one of the largest in the country. My employer was the state's largest healthcare system. If I left, would I ever have the chance of getting a job in the state? What if I am told to leave my ID badge and take my personal belongings immediately? How would I explain this to my children or my parents, especially my dad? I worked hard and sacrificed much to get to this level. My dad was so proud of me. He always said, "Just keep that job and retire to get your pension. It's hard out here. You need to just lay low and keep that job." This was the lesson I had been taught by my parents — get a good job and work hard. I love them both. They inspired me to work hard. However, I was unhappy. I was unfulfilled. The problems were numerous. I was on the verge of a marital separation. I was totally disconnected from my children. I spent more time in the office and at meetings than with my family. I was walking around mentally, physically, and spiritually drained. I suffered from migraines, hypertension, and stress.

But was not this the American Dream? I worked so hard to earn this title, this position. This was the income earning I thought would make me happy. This was the window office with a view that I had only dreamed about. But wait, is this not what I was supposed to be doing? My calling was not being fulfilled. I was empty. I was frustrated. I was fearful. I was called.

Fear of failure kept me from answering the call on my life. Fear of who wouldn't believe in me. Fear of who wouldn't like me. Fear of success. Fear of God's promises. Fear of falling. Fear of power; fear of disappointments. Fear of abandonment. Fear of being me. Fear of rejection. Fear of the voices that would say, "Who do you think you are?" Have you ever experienced any of these fears? I have struggled with all of them and many more.

I began to realize that fear is false evidence appearing real, and began to understand that everything I was afraid had no power over me until I gave it power. Everything I feared was external, and my calling and purpose were internal. The external could not hinder or stop what was inside of me. No matter how much I tried to run from and avoid the call, it followed me. God's grace and mercy followed me. All the external factors could not stop the call. The call was from deep down on the inside.

My entire life, I tried to fit in. I desired to a part of the girls and fit in with the crowd. But I never really felt comfortable or fit in. Each time I compromised my calling to fit in, I felt empty and unfulfilled. Fear of saying "no" to having sex with him. Fear of not being a part of the crowd. Fear of saying no to them. All for what? I was pleasing others and dying inside. I constantly had this tug-of-war going on inside of me. On one side of me, I felt invincible, courageous, legendary, beautiful, and intelligent. The other side of me was cautious, timid, sensitive, reserved, inadequate, and afraid of being hurt. Afraid of what people would say. Many times, when I would begin to step into my calling, people would say, "Who does she think she is?" Not really knowing who I was, I played it "small" and allowed other people's opinions to dictate what I did and who I did it with. Deep inside, I knew I was a queen. You see I had a father who taught me I was an African queen, standing on the shoulders of my ancestors. I had a mother who told be to respect myself and others would do the same. However, there was a world that told me I was too black, too big, too loud, and certainly didn't have enough money to measure up.

When you walk out of the four walls of what you call home into the streets as a young girl, you have to make some decisions. Do I believe what those who love me have told me? Do I follow my heart and true identity? Or do I follow the crowd or believe what the teachers, media, and culture say about me? There were many times as a young girl when I followed my heart and vividly remember people looking at me with contempt or laughing at me. These reactions caused me to pull back and become fearful of what others would think. But what if I really walked in my true identity and demonstrated exactly who I was and who I was called to be? What's the worst thing that could happen?

Fear affected the choices I made. This fear caused me to play small. Have you had this great idea and the moment you share it with someone, they shot it down? You went from 100 mph to a complete stop in 30 seconds. It's like being on a roller coaster — you're so excited when you get to the peak; you have this awesome idea or plan and you share it with someone whose opinion you value. They don't agree or believe in your idea, and you immediately plunge to the bottom. All your hopes and desires were tied to that one person's belief in you. Has that ever happened to you? It happened to me many times, and it affected my faith in myself.

I had the dream of being a lawyer and helping people. All throughout high school, I had a desire to become a lawyer. I remember the first time I shared it with my mother. I had an idea of going to a large university until the day my mom said, "We don't have money for you to go to those types of schools." I was heartbroken. So, I downgraded my dream, went to a community college, and pursued a degree in nursing. I made this choice simply because it was a career in demand. This continued my pattern of "playing it small," taking the easy way out, and seeing myself as being normal or mediocre, all while feeling and believing I was grand and made different on purpose. I wish I'd had the courage and the faith to stand up and say, "No, I am going after my dream. We don't have the money? I will find the money." But no, I played it safe, and looked for a career that I could complete quickly and while on a budget.

My parents meant well. They worked hard — especially my mom. She was a single mother who sacrificed a lot for her children. My dad worked his way through community colleges and received his degree while working and trying to provide for his children. My mom earned her Master's degree while in her 60's. All they knew was to work, make a living, and do the best you can. I appreciate the work ethic I gained from both of them. However, I always knew that I was called to be more and to do more than work a 9-5, earn a pension, and retire comfortably. I knew there was more. I had faith that there was more.

I remember my 3rd grade teacher, Mrs. Mazza. She was a heavy-set Italian woman — very round and jolly with a beautiful smile. She was so inspiring. She always made me feel like I could do anything. I remember reading *Charlotte's*

Web in her class. I was so engulfed in that story that I felt I wanted to live on a farm and milk cows and feed pigs. I recall how special, smart, and beautiful she made me feel because normally, I didn't feel that way. Before meeting Mrs. Mazza, I thought my hair was too nappy, my nose was too big, and my skin was too dark. She was the first person outside of my family that boosted my self-confidence. So much so that 30 years later, I remember her. My 3rd grade teacher made me feel powerful, capable, and courageous. I have decided that I want to do the same for every young girl I come in contact with. Can you recall one person that made you feel special? Is there one person who made you feel like you could do anything? We all need someone to encourage us and stimulate our faith, not our fears.

Today's society doesn't empower, encourage, or inspire our girls. Many girls become women that lack courage and inspiration, so the cycle continues. I want to be one of the ones to change that. I want to do what Mrs. Mazza did for me for so many girls and women. The funny thing about me is my resolve. I was always able to make something happen in any situation or circumstance. You give me lemons, I'll make lemonade. Whatever hand I am dealt with, I will make something happen. The calling on my life always allowed me to find favor in spite of my mess. God's promises will be fulfilled. Faith has the power to overcome fear.

It didn't matter that I ended up pregnant at 18 years old. It didn't matter that I had to drop out of college and work a full-time job to pay rent, day care, and provide for my son. God's favor and calling still allowed me to work, get promotions, provide for my son, and return back to college to get my nursing degree. It didn't matter that I discovered while 6 month's pregnant that my son's father was selling drugs. Fear of losing him caused me to turn a blind eye to what he was doing. Fear of losing him made me not inquire where the money was coming from. Fear of being alone would have me settle for less than I deserved. Are you settling for less than you deserve?

It didn't matter that I would have to be a single mom and raise my son alone while his father was in prison. None of this would change the calling I had on my life.

The obstacles that come into our lives show us how we can overcome. You don't develop your muscles and strength by sitting comfortably on the sidelines. You develop your courage and strength by lifting weights and pushing past the fear, hurts, pain, and disappointments. The wonderful thing about life is that it's a journey. There is a process. If you allow the process to develop you and not deter you, you will see victory and achieve greatness. Let me be clear: the process can be painful and often rough. Process causes progression and development, but only if you allow it. I say if you *allow* it because it's easy to give up during the process. It's tempting to take the easy way out and skip a step or two. It is tempting to choose fear over faith. There are no short cuts in process. Anything you try to skip will be repeated. The lessons must be learned. The beautiful thing about being called is that "all things work together for our good." What the enemy sent or meant to destroy us becomes the stepping stone to get us to answer the call.

The calling does not make you exempt from hardship, trials, and temptations. The calling allows you to still rise and bring other people up with you when you rise. I am learning daily that "it's not about you, Boo!" I am called to this journey to help others. I went through that test to help others pass the test and perhaps avoid the test all together. I want to help others skip grades and accelerate the process.

Life is precious, and life is so short. I believe I wasted many years not walking in my true identity and not answering the call upon my life. I have a niece that died at 23. My brother (her father) died at 44. There are so many classmates and colleagues that passed away way too soon. So, the goal is to optimize the time I have left and leave a legacy of courage, inspiration, and motivation that will last years, decades, and generations after I am gone. That's my calling. Whether the legacy is in my children, with the young people I meet, or the business owners that don't give up and excel because of me and see the difference in their lives — that's the calling. If it's just one person reading this book that says, "I will answer the call and have an impact on my community," then it was all worth the process. It was worth every tear I cried, it was worth every sleepless night, and it was worth every struggle and lesson. As the song says, "If I can help somebody as I pass along, then my living shall not be in vain."

Have you ever felt like there was much more to life? I did each and every day. Every time I saw a friend or a love one had passed way too soon, my desire and discernment to answer the call became bigger. I realized that I was sacrificing way too much. My peace, my gift, my love, and my calling were all at stake. Life is way too short to waste a day or an hour not being true to your calling or your purpose. The day I answered the call and surrendered, I began to open my life, my time, and my heart to my calling is the day I felt joy, peace, and liberation.

It was a tough decision, I must admit. I'd worked so hard for one thing, only to realize and face the reality that it was not all that's there for me. God has so much more in store for you. That's when you have to walk by faith and not fear. It's an extreme leap of faith to walk away from the "good" to walk into the "great." I had to no longer fear their faces. I had to walk by faith and not by sight. Did you ever have to do something that you know would not make sense to anyone but you. They say the enemy of being great is being comfortable.

> *"Don't be afraid to give up the good and go for the great."* — Steve Prefonaine

My story may not be like most. I was not unemployed, suffering from hardships, or down on my luck. I had tasted success in my career and in my business. However, there is much more in store. I don't have all the answers. No one does. That's why life is a journey. There are bumps, turns, twists, pot holes, stops signs, yield signs, speed bumps, and green lights. I am grateful for the signs that have led me to answer my call and forsake the good to go for the great. One day, when I was in my transition period, torn about what to do, I recall my mom saying, "You're gonna be alright. God has more for you to do. You would not leave on your own. He's forcing you to move."

Have you ever had to make a tough decision? A decision that you knew would influence everyone you loved? Most people would not understand your decision. You know you had to make it the decision — the choice was yours and only yours to make. The calling is yours and only yours to answer. Will you answer the call?

You are an Overcomer
Anana Phifer-Derilhomme

"When we tackle obstacles, we find hidden reserves of courage and resilience we did not know we had. And it is only when we are faced with failure do we realize that these resources were always there within us. We only need to find them and move on with our lives."
— A. P. J. Abdul Kalam

I had to believe in myself. Once I began to walk in my own calling, passion, and gifting, I felt alive. You will know and feel "it." When you are walking in your calling, you will feel amazing. It's a feeling I find hard to explain. Believe in it. Own it. It takes courage to believe in yourself. It takes courage to be different and have faith that you are good enough. Actually, you are better than good — you are great! Say it loud and proud! "I AM GREAT!" Remind yourself every day. There will be numerous situations, challenges, and people that will question and try to minimize your greatness. So always start with the affirmation that I AM GREAT! I AM CALLED!

Yes, you are great! There is greatness inside of us waiting to emerge. You just have to tap into your greatness. You have to discover your greatness. It's there. It's in every one of us. We all have greatness inside of us. Here's the secret. It's hard being great! There will be many obstacles and challenges to you achieving and sustaining your greatness. So, let's just put that out there right now. Don't be surprised — you should expect them. When things are going smoothly, I am looking over my shoulder saying to myself, "What's about to happen?" I know that with every accomplishment, there will be adversity and obstacles.

We all know Michael Jordan. He is probably one of the world's most successful basketball players. He put it this way: "If you're trying to achieve, there will be roadblocks. I've had them; everybody has had them. But obstacles don't have to stop you. If you run into a wall, don't turn around and give up. Figure out how to climb it, go through it, or work around it."

Get used to the roadblocks and opposition. I am learning to thrive against the obstacles. I let them fuel my fire. They encourage me to push even harder. Again, we are developing our muscles. Our muscles will not develop under comfortable conditions. Our strength and muscles are developed as we stretch and stress them. So, don't be dismayed when obstacles come. Stay solution-minded and always look for ways to overcome them. Say to yourself, "This is not going to stop me. I am going to actually work even harder and smarter to make it happen!"

You are an overcomer. You don't let anything stop you. Be unstoppable and be successful. There are three steps I have used to overcome and answer the call:

1. **Decide.** "Wanting something is not enough. You must hunger for it. Your motivation must be absolutely compelling in order to overcome the obstacles that will invariably come your way." — Les Brown

It starts with your decision. You have to decide to move forward and be who you are called to be. You will use your gift and talents to discover and fulfill your dreams and purpose. 99% of the time, this will enhance someone else's life. You see, you do have a choice. There are alternatives for you. You can stay where you are. You can keep doing what you are doing. You can keep hanging around the same people, doing the same things. Do you want to say, "I wish I could've and would have?" or you can say, "I am called and I will walk in my calling." God gave you these gifts. He made you this way for a reason. You will develop, pursue, and contribute to your calling.

2. **Commit**. "The gateways to wisdom and learning are always open, and more and more I am choosing to walk through them. Barriers, blocks, obstacles, and problems are personal teachers giving me the opportunity to move out of the past and into the Totality of Possibilities." — Louise L. Hay

You have to make a commitment to the calling. Once you decide, you have to commit to your decision. There will be opposition. You will have to get uncomfortable. You will have to face your fears. I am certain you may lose some people along the way. This can be one of the most difficult areas. Many people around you now are used to you being exactly who you have been. They are comfortable with you being comfortable. Your family and friends may know you, but not know or recognize your calling. Prayerfully, you do have some family and friends that do recognize and appreciate your calling. I am blessed to have my mom and some close friends that recognized it, even sometimes before I did. Stay connected to those that do. Let them know that you are committed your calling, and that you appreciate them for believing in you and seeing you. Unfortunately, many people don't walk in their calling. Could you imagine if we lived in a world where more people walked in their calling? Just imagine what our world would look like. Make a commitment that no matter who believes in you that you will answer the call and stay committed. To commit is to fully dedicate yourself to something. Another definition is to entrust, especially for safekeeping. We have to entrust our lives to the calling and the process. Commit and know that you are going to embark on an amazing journey. It will be amazing — not easy. I wish I could tell you once you commit, everything will work out and things will just fall into place. That is not the case. Your commitment will be tested. Your will and determination will be tested. It will be worth it.

"There are plenty of difficult obstacles in your path. Don't allow yourself to become one of them." — Ralph Marston

3. **Take action.** Once you've made the decision and committed to it, it's time to take action. Let's move forward. Let's find out what you need to do and who we need to do it with. There are people assigned to assist you. Look for people that will help you as you develop. Look for people who have answered their calling and are

successfully taking action. Partner with these people. There are people assigned to help you and there are people you are assigned to help. Action is defined as the process of doing something, especially when dealing with a problem or difficulty.

> *"Action without vision in only passing time, vision without action is merely day dreaming but vision with action can change the world."*
> — Nelson Mandela

It's time to move forward. Take the step towards your calling. Start living it. Start feeding it. Start practicing it. Start walking in it. I have an acronym that will be helpful as you answer the call:

A — Assert yourself. Put yourself where you are being led. Go where you are appreciated, developed, and inspired. Be around people that enjoy you, encourage you, and inspire you. You will have to step up and step out. You will have to be bold and brave.

C — Confidence. Be confident in yourself, your calling, and your gifts. Many people confuse confidence with cockiness. You don't have to be cocky to be confident. Just be clear and aware of who you are and what you are called to do. There will be many people that don't understand your calling. But let them watch God move on your behalf and watch God use you for His glory. My confidence comes from my faith in God. I am confident in the one who called me rather than in my own ability.

T — Timely. Don't waste any more time. We all have the same 24 hours in a day. What do you do with the time? How do you use your time wisely? Be mindful of how you spend your time and who you spend it with. Time is fleeting, and you must plan your time and a lot time to rest, relate, relax, and rejuvenate. I believe this book will help you value your time and prioritize what really matters.

I — Identity. Find your own identity — who you are and who you're called to be — and be just that. Don't let anyone change, mold, or alter that identity. You have all you need inside of you to be who you are. Your identity is who you are and, more importantly, what make you different. What sets you apart from everyone else is your identity. Embrace your identity. Your calling is contingent on your identity. Once you determine your identity and answer the call, you will become unstoppable. Once you walk in your identity and calling, others will see it. Others will be drawn to it. Let's embrace our identity. Let's embrace what makes us unique. Your identity is your winning hand. No one can be you. No one can do it like you. People are waiting for you to be you and walk in your calling.

O — Opportunity. "Life's up and downs provide windows of opportunity to determine your values and goals. Think of using all obstacles as stepping stones to build the life you want" —Marsha Sinetar.

Take every opportunity to use your gifts and talents. Obstacles become opportunities to learn more about yourself and others and help you develop your talents. As you answer the calling, opportunities will always present themselves. You just need to be sensitive and aware of the opportunity. Stay ready so you don't have to get ready. Opportunities can turn your weaknesses into strengths. The same things that used to annoy me don't bother me anymore, because I have answered the call and know this too shall pass.

N — Needs. Meet the needs of others. Find people who need what you have. We are not called for our own pleasures and self-fulfillment. We are called to help meet the needs of people. Your calling maybe to work with the elderly, young people, people in a foreign land, homeless children, pregnant women, or men and women in prison. The needs are limitless. Those that are willing to answer the call and meet the needs of others are sometimes few. I know that if you are reading this book, you are someone who wants to help meet the needs of others by answering the call and taking action.

    I discovered my calling to become a coach and speaker as I developed my jewelry business and grew in my career. Oftentimes, people would just open up and share their challenges and obstacles with me. I became a good listener, which makes me able to coach others though the challenge and encourage them to discover the opportunity to succeed even in the face of a challenging situation. A coach is an "instructor/trainer." Oxford University used slang for a tutor who "carries" a student through an exam. It's someone whose job is to teach people to improve at a sport, skill, or school subject. We all need someone to carry us through a test. Imagine how much further we would be if we had someone who taught us how to improve our skills and talents? What a blessing it is to have someone who believes in us and will work with us as we become the very best we can be. Remember my third-grade teacher, Mrs. Mazza? She was my teacher, but also a coach for me, even at that young age. I want to be that person and have that impact on a third grader, a third-year college student, a thirty-year-old, and even a seventy-three-year-old. That's my calling. I realized that I am blessed girl. We are all blessed to be a blessing to someone else. I have the ability to see the possibilities and opportunities that are available once we open our hearts and minds to them.

You can do it! You would not have a calling to something that you could not achieve, accomplish, or provide. You have what it takes, but it's going to take all you've got! Larry Myler, a Forbes contributor, says, "As I look back on all the ventures I have watched, heard of, read about or participated in, on common entrepreneurial trait that keeps showing up as the key to success (or failure): The trait is tenacity (or lack thereof)." Tenacity is the quality or fact of being able to grip something firmly. You have to grab a hold to the calling and hold tight to it. Hold tight to the calling and don't let anyone talk you out of it. Don't let any circumstance cause you to not answer the call!

When you answer the call, it is going to take faith.

"Faith is taking the first step even when you don't see the whole stair case." — Dr Martin Luther King Jr.

You won't have all the answers. You won't have all the plans and directions. You are simply answering the call. You have to move forward and answer the call. No one has all the answers. You have to answer the call that no one else hears. You have to have the vision that no one else sees. If you don't, who will? It's your calling. It's your purpose. It will take faith. Consider it this way. You know where you are going — you just don't know exactly how you are going to get there. Your final destination is to live a life full and die empty. I don't want to live a life of regrets and what if's. I am going to live my best life now. How about you?

We all use a GPS almost every day. GPS stands for a global positional system, and it is quickly becoming an integrative part of our society. It is a worldwide radio-navigation system formed from a constellation of 24 satellites and their ground stations. We rely on this system to get us where we need to go. I have actually used it to travel from the United States to Canada. I have so much trust in this application that I let it guide me into another country and get me around as I traveled. Consider how much confidence we place on this application. Wow! How much faith do I have in this device and technology? Can we have that same amount of trust and faith in God? Do we trust our maker to get us to our final destination? Do we trust Him enough to answer the call? Do we trust God enough to guide us step by step? God knows exactly where you stand today. He knows exactly where and how you need to get there. Last, but not least, He has equipped you with all you need to get there.

The biggest difference and hardest part for us to accept is this: the GPS will allow you to preview the directions, turns, and highways you will travel on, but our spiritual GPS does not have that preview option. I like to call it my "Godly positional system." There are no preview steps. It would be great if we have a GPS that says, "Today make this turn, travel this number of miles, take this exit," and so on. Wouldn't this be amazing? But it doesn't work like that. We must have faith and yield our trust and will to God to lead and guide us. After all, He is the one who called us. We can certainly trust him to guide our steps. We have to answer the call and allow God to provide the step-by-step directions we need to take to get there. If we can put our trust in technology that is man-made and full of errors, updates, and hiccups, how much more trust and faith can we put in God to guide us with the steps to fully answer the calling and be all that He has called us to be?

We all need someone to help keep us moving forward. We all need someone to encourage us and help keep us on track. We all need someone. There may be different people at different stages of our life. I am available to coach and train those that need a voice to help strengthen your core to fulfill your purpose and answer the call to live your best life. You need to be careful who you share your calling with. Most people don't understand the calling on your life. It's even harder for someone to understand or appreciate the calling if they themselves have not answered their own calling. We have already determined that most people don't answer the call, or even take the time to recognize the call. But that's not going to be you. You are going to live your best life by answering the call that has been placed on your life. You will use all your gifts and talents to live a blessed life and be a blessing to others. I would love to work with you and hear about your journey to answering the call and living your best life.

Anana Phifer-Derilhomme

Anana Phifer-Derilhomme is a motivational speaker, business development coach and National and International Expansion leader with Traci Lynn Jewelry. She has over 17 years' experience in Healthcare Administration, and an award-winning career in direct sales, team expansion, leadership training, and coaching.

Anana is a wife and mother to 3 awesome sons. She has a gift to inspire and the knowledge to direct and develop others in business. She truly enjoys seeing others reach their full potential in life. Anana considers herself a "blessed girl" with a purpose to help inspire and encourage others to fulfill their dreams. She has proven success strategies that help others to acknowledge and develop their greatness.

"As the butterfly evolves, so do we as God's chosen vessels to live a life of Passion and Purpose."

Anana has a passionate purpose of helping others believe and achieve their goals and dreams. "I have made it one of life's mission to help others identify their calling, identity, and purpose early on in life in order to maximize their potential, their impact, and to win BIG in the journey of life."

Contact information:

msblessedgirl@yahoo.com
www.tracilynnjewelry.net/7087
Twitter: @AnanaP_blingz
Instagram: @ananablings
Facebook: Anana Phifer-Derilhomme

Midnight
Robin Cody Smith

"The song is ended, but the melody lingers on..."
— Irving Berlin

It was the Friday before Mother's Day. Earlier in the week, I called my son. As usual, I left him my famous message: "Mommy loves you."

Richard Ellsworth Smith is my only child. He was educated in the Montessori school system starting at the age of 4. He was a brilliant child. Well, I guess many parents would call their children smart, bright, or even intelligent, but Richard was above average. I attributed his intelligence to the exposure that he had as a child.

Though his grandparents were concerned about him attending a learning institution so young, I guaranteed them that if it was challenging for him or if he was not comfortable, then I would remove him from the school. They were unaware that I was also teaching him at home. Whether it was the alphabet, math, reading, or spelling, after each teaching experience, I would ask my son one question. His reply was always the same.

The question was, "Who am I?" With a smile on his face, his faithful response was, "Mom, you are the world's greatest teacher." Yes, I taught him to say that, too.

He was the child that could answer many of the questions on the game show, *Jeopardy*. He could answer mathematical problems without calculator, paper, or pencil.

I remembered writing a paper for college while my son played with a new toy. He asked me to assist him with the assembly of the toy. Honestly, I was in the momentum of completing the paper, so my son's new Transformer gadget was not a priority.

But to encourage my child, I picked up the toy. I handled it for about three minutes and returned it to him. I informed him that I was unable to assemble it. His reply to me at age 5 was, "Mommy, can you take your time and use your brains?" Well, how could I respond to his statement? I did just as he requested. I took my time, read the instructions, and assembled the toy. He was a deep thinker.

My son graduated from West Chester University in West Chester, PA. Upon graduating, he decided to make Pennsylvania his home state.

I was confident that he would return my call.

Greek Class
After completing my workday in the federal government and following up with the team members in my direct selling organization, I looked forward to my Greek class.

But my Thursday night Greek class was really different. I had about six more classes to take to complete the semester. Koine Greek was part of the curriculum for my Bachelor's degree in theology.

It was the first time that the teacher spoke about death. I would normally have some clever words for the teacher. After all, we were all doing our best to speak and understand the basics of Biblical Greek. But tonight was different.

The death topic had nothing to do with our Greek studies at all. The topic just did not fit. We were not learning new vocabulary. There was no correlation with what we were studying. My fellow students and I somberly listened until he was finished. We said our good nights as each student journeyed to their perspective abodes.

Home

It was a calm, peaceful May evening. I drove from the city to my home in the suburbs. Once home, I followed my normal routine. I was preparing to say goodnight to Thursday when my phone rang.

This was not normal. Who could be calling me at midnight? The ringing phone appeared to launch into my hands as I reached for it. The caller was my son's father. It is the call that no parent wants to give or receive.

The words he shared changed our lives forever. He said Richard was gone. I replied, "Gone where?" A plethora of thoughts permeated my mind. Was he moving from Pennsylvania? Did he elope? Was he on his way to New York?

I was not expecting the response that I received from his father as he shared the details that he knew. The unimaginable happened. A car accident claimed the life on my only child.

Was there a defect in the previously-owned car that my son purchased a few days earlier? I cried — I am crying now as I am writing this chapter — and declared that the car dealership better not be responsible for my son's early departure.

After I hung up the phone, I screamed to the top of my voice. The volume of my vocal cords could have shattered glass, but it definitely woke up my neighbor. I called my family and texted some friends. One of my brothers kept telling me that it was not true. He said, "He is the good one." I fully understood my brother. My son was quite different than his cousins. He was the only one that graduated from college; he was the only one that did not have the "street life.

Did my Greek teacher become spiritually aware that death was a needed discussion because a student would have an unexpected experience? My Greek teacher and my son's father shared the death topic that did not fit in my life. It was not a topic for discussion. Death could not be associated with my child. Yet, the unexpected death topic was rapidly becoming my reality.

The midnight call had no mercy. The midnight call was a thief in the night. The midnight call was the call that no parent wants to give or receive.

It was midnight. My son was gone. It was the Friday before Mother's Day! How could this be happening? What could I have done to prevent it? How do I make this horrible new reality go away? I am a single parent without a child. Children should outlive their parents.

A young lady informed my family that she and my son were texting each other in the moments leading up to his death. She said suddenly, the texting stopped. She did not receive a response from my son. My son was texting while driving. He lost control of the car. The car crashed into a tree. My son died upon impact.

The National Safety Council reports that "Many distractions exist while driving, but cell phones are a top distraction because so many drivers use them for long periods of time each day. Almost everyone has seen a driver distracted by a cell phone, but when you are the one distracted, you often don't realize that driver is you."

My intelligent, kind-hearted son made an incorrect decision that changed our lives forever. Parents are not supposed to bury their children, but his untimely death changed everything.

Unexpected Loss

An unexpected loss is one that has no points of reference, or no clues to indicate an imminent loss. It can lead to a place of mental immobility, where moving forward can be a challenge or even seem impossible.

An unexpected loss could be:

The loss of a job.
The loss of faith in a spouse due to infidelity.
The loss of a baby during the birth process.
The loss of a business partner due to embezzlement.
The loss of a loved one, family member, or friend.

This list is not meant to be exhaustive. These are some of the unexpected losses I've observed in those I've coached.

The United States had no points of reference that a terrorist plot could be successful in attacking the country. Yet, on September 11, 2001, the unexpected occurred and the World Trade Center in New York was no more, and thousands of people lost their lives.

An unexpected loss is the most devastating to deal with because there are no valid indicators. You can't prepare for it, which makes it that much more difficult to process, navigate, and comprehend.

No More Responsibilities

I built a successful direct sales business while working full-time in the federal government. Actually, I represented the top 2% of the company. I skillfully led my team in producing over $300,000 in sales for several years. I duplicated myself in the team. I mastered the ability to produce a viable additional stream of income for myself and for others in the industry.

I continued operating my business for a few months after the tragedy to prove to myself and others that I could still be successful. Yet, I made the decision to give up my lucrative business. I decided that I needed to grieve, and I did not want any more responsibilities.

The only reason that I did not leave the government job is because I was not pressured in returning to work, and I was not directly working with the public. I was able to continue doing my job without putting my grief on display. There was no pressure from the direct sales organization, either. Actually, I felt a great compassion from the entire company. I remembered the day I made the call to the corporate offices to give my departure reason. The director of my division reiterated that I did not have to make the decision to leave, and they would work with me according to my pace.

My son would often accompany me on business appointments (an element of flexibility in direct sales) as my assistant. I always thought that my son was a key part in my increasing sales. My customers loved him. They always complemented me on his great behavior, and on how he would help me and them with a smile on his face.

In retrospect, I unconsciously gave up the business because my son and my business were so closely related that it was challenging to have one and not the other. I was responsible for my son, but my son is gone, and I just did not want to be responsible for anyone or anything else.

After my conversation with the director, I sent an email to memorialize my departure conversation. In the email, I declared that I would return.

Grief Intensified
I unintentionally intensified my grief by relinquishing my business. The loss of extra income from the business was significant. I found myself dealing with two losses simultaneously.

Truth: Do not give up anything while dealing with an unexpected loss. Things that seem like burdens may actually be what's keeping you going.

Faith
My faith community was instrumental in providing a place of normalcy.

Truth: Return to normal as quickly as possible.

Grief is a personal experience, and it can manifest in different ways. The maintenance process for an unexpected loss can be a lifelong journey because you really never "get over" an unexpected loss. Yet, it will become more manageable over time as you learn to accept it, cope with it, and live within that loss.

How to Overcome an Unexpected Loss
Robin Cody Smith

"You never know how strong you are until being strong is the only choice you have." — Bob Marley

During the aftermath of the unexpected loss of my son, I journaled my progress. As I viewed the journal, I realized that I created a 12-step system that assisted me through the process. A system that is also assisting others that experienced an unexpected loss.

I do not have a PhD, nor do I have any specific medical training in unexpected losses, but I have personal, first-hand experience. The best teacher is one that has experience in the field or subject. Unfortunately, I'm a subject matter expert on unexpected loss. C.S. Lewis said it best: "Experience: that most brutal of teachers. But you learn, my God do you learn."

Here are 5 steps of my 12-step system to assist with an unexpected loss as you answer the call on your life.

1. Accept that a loss has occurred.
This does not mean to accept how the loss occurred, but it does mean to get a grip on the fact that there is a loss.

2. Find and take comfort in your faith community.
The faith community allows you to be built up from the inside out on a weekly basis. If you are not associated

with a faith community, you may consider joining a meditation group.

3. Know and embrace your tears and grief triggers.

Tears are important part of the healing process. You could have unexpected tears in non-traditional circumstances. I was printing the program for my son's final services. There were some challenges with the printing company. The corrected programs were given to me for free. I said to the person assisting me, "I guess this is my Mother's Day gift." I immediately began to cry as I ran out of the establishment.

Grief triggers are temporary. As time goes on, it will become easier to go through your day without unexpected grief triggers, though they can still occur. I learned about the benefits of tears while preparing the eulogy for my 94-year-old grand uncle. There are 3 types of tears: basal, reflex, and emotional.

- Basal is a lubricating tear; it is produced slowly and steadily throughout the day. The basal tear is constantly present in the eye, which ensures that the cornea is always wet and nourished.

- Reflex tears serve as a kind of emergency response to flood the eye when it is suddenly irritated or injured. These tears are mostly water — onions, pepper spray, or tear gas will cause the reflex tears to form.

- Emotional tears have more protein than the basal and reflex tears. High levels of happy or sad emotions cause this tear to form. This tear is formed to stabilize the mood as quickly as possible along with other physical reactions such as increased heart rate and slower breathing.

Emotional tears also contain higher levels of stress hormones and natural pain killers. Research suggests that the production of emotional tears helps the body to feel calmer and less emotional afterwards. You must freely use the emotional tears as often as needed, as they are designed for such a time as this.

4. Drink, eat, and sleep.
Water is not my favorite beverage, yet it is what the body needs — especially when there is an unexpected loss. Dehydration, even to the level of being chronic, can be a side effect of an unexpected loss. Dehydration will cause additional emotional strains, such as headaches, confusion, fever, chills, fainting, sluggishness, and elevated blood pressure. Drink water to stay hydrated. Strive to drink at least one bottle of water, and continually increase your water intake.

Avoid all alcoholic beverages. For many people, drinking is a typical way to deal with the aftermath of an unexpected loss, but it only prolongs the grieving process. Drink a glass of water instead to keep your mind clear and focused.

Eating and maintaining a healthy appetite appears to be more challenging for women. Men are also challenged in this area, but they appear to recover much quicker. Some people eat for comfort, while others lose their desire to eat altogether. Grief does strange and unexpected things to the body.

An older woman told me that I was going to feel an emptiness or strangeness in the bottom of my belly. She was correct. I had the experience just as she described. Food was not on my mind, nor did I have urges to eat. My appetite was gone.

Food is the fuel that your body absolutely requires during times of an unexpected loss. You can start with small meal, but start as soon as possible.

The body is a state of stress because of the unexpected loss, and it needs to go to bed early. Even if you are finding it a challenge to fall asleep, go to bed early, turn the light off (if you can), and lie down, because your body is exhausted — even if you do not feel tired.

Tip: avoid caffeinated drinks or any substance that could unnaturally keep you from sleep.

You're dealing with events that are beyond your control, so focus on areas that you can control, such as getting rest, staying hydrated, and eating well.

5. Time, and lots of it.

I know it is painful. You had no warning. There was no way that you could have prepared yourself for this unexpected loss. I honestly know how you feel.

A famous Geoffrey Chaucer quote is, "Time heals all wounds." Time will not fill the void of your loss. But, time will heal the wounds that are associated with the pain, even though you will have the scars as a reminder for life.

Allow time to work in your favor. Draw upon your inner strength and strive to get by, even if it's just moment to moment at first.

New Normal

You will not return to the place you were prior to the unexpected loss. Why? Because you are not the same. The adjustments, the adapting to your new realization, and the experience itself prohibits you from being the same person that you were prior to the unexpected loss.

I was putting together a women's conference. Though I was the keynote speaker, the team was searching for additional support speakers. One person that the team found was the wife of a pastor of a mega church in Michigan. She was not available to attend the event, yet she was a part of the direct selling organization that I left. We spoke about the possibility of a future date for her to attend the event; we also talked about the direct selling organization.

I was not sure if the economy was right. I was not sure if I was ready yet, but I took the Nike attitude of "Just Do It." I restarted my business in the direct selling industry.

My resurrected business's challenge was rebuilding in an area where so many people knew of my prior success. I felt like I had to explain the reason for my absence in the field. I did not want to replay my tragedy. I did not want people to be sad or feel sorry for me.

Yet, I learned that the unexpected loss that I went through was assisting so many people that were also attempting to cope with various unexpected losses in their lives. The human spirit is profoundly resilient. The inner strength I discovered allowed me to walk others through the healing process.

I was gaining energy to ultimately produce (GETUP) once again in the industry. Within four short months, I regained the leadership position. Once again, I represented the top 2% of the company. I was stronger than I was the first time. I reached levels that were not achieved previously in my business.

Though I am licensed in ministry and I speak on various secular and faith-based platforms, my message and presence after my unexpected loss were empowered by a new inner fire. My new normal was similar to the normal prior to the unexpected loss of my son, but it was not the same. The new normal is the place where you will flourish in your calling.

Whether I was in church, at home, working my business, or at my job, people would come to me and ask me questions about business and various life challenges. I would give my advice, resources, and/or recommendations.

The continual confirmation of my calling was reinforced each time a person would return to me and share the success that was achieved because of my unconventional consultation.

My calling is to provide training and personal development through coaching, mentoring, and business strategies. It can be seen in my vocation, business, ministry, and entrepreneurial ventures. My son called me "the world's greatest teacher." Well, I'm here today teaching and helping others answer the call on their life and move to their next level of success.

You have no control over unexpected losses, but you can control your response to it. No matter the circumstances that you face in life, you must operate in your calling. Experiencing an unexpected loss can leave you feeling hopeless — like you should just give up on your dreams, hopes, and aspirations. I'm living proof that when you operate in your calling, it's never too late to reach the next level of your success. Today, I honor the memory of my son's too-short life. My actions and experiences create a living monument to what his life meant.

A major element of living your best life is achieved through identifying the call and answering it! In closing, I leave this word with you: "bounce-back." I restarted the business that I gave up during the tragedy. The business grew faster and stronger the second time around. I also opened a second business that on the rise. By the way, the wife of the pastor of the mega church in Michigan spoke at the conference three years later.

I believe that this chapter will be a catalyst for you to start Gaining Energy to Ultimately Produce (GETUP).

You can stay in contact with me and share your progress by joining the Facebook Community: The Next Level Success.

For free and additional resources, visit: www.RobinCodySmith.com

Robin Cody Smith

Robin Cody Smith, aka The Next Level Specialist, is the founder of GETUP LLC.

As an acclaimed author, certified coach, mentor, speaker, and corporate trainer, Robin empowers entrepreneurs, employers, and employees to reach the next level of their professional success.

As a leader in the direct sales industry, ministry, and government, Robin has identified common threads that are missing in many businesses, teams, and leaders that provide insights, techniques, and strategies necessary in achieving upward mobility in business and in life.

GETUP (Gaining Energy to Ultimately Produce) LLC is a training and development company that offers a range of innovative coaching, proven business strategies, corporate training, and online products.

Website: www.RobinCodySmith.com
Facebook: The Next Level Specialist
LinkedIn: Robin Cody Smith

Made in the USA
Middletown, DE
28 April 2017